Maiden Voyage is an apt title for Pat Gerber's first book of prose, a mixture of fiction and non-fiction in which women – maidens, wives, mothers – are often striking out on uncharted seas of experience. If the situations are familiar – teenage rebellions, rocky marriages, coping with illness, the loss of someone loved – the reactions to them are unexpectedly adventurous. Pat Gerber's women are determined creatures, and they battle: often against physical odds – a fear of diving, a difficult climb – in the Scottish landscape she describes with affectionate clarity. The challenges they set themselves are seen in the context of a living society, a society Pat Gerber believes can change, and must be awakened to change: the process has to start within the hearts and minds of individuals. She sees how difficult this process is and how tempting it is to accept the status quo, and she laces her narratives with laughter. These are the stories of your family, your neighbours, your country – and Pat Gerber tells them with vivid accuracy and warmth.

FOR GWYNNETH, MY FRIEND

Edited by Robyn Marsack

Cover painting 'Catch' by Lesley Banks

Jacket design by Jill Gerber

Wood Engravings by Heather Wilson

Heather Wilson was born 1962 in Newcastle, studied printmaking at Sunderland Poly, won joint award from Northern Arts to illustrate The Book Of Exeter Riddles, in 1989-90 printed 1,000 of Thomas Bewick's original wood engravings for Newcastle Central Library, and in 1991 gave birth to Simon.

# MAIDEN VOYAGE

## PAT GERBER

Kailyards Press

First published in Great Britain by
Kailyards Press, 148 West Regent Street, Glasgow G2 2RQ
FAX: 041 248 1322
Copyright © Pat Gerber 1992

BRITISH LIBRARY CATALOGUING-IN-PUBLICATION DATA
A catalogue record for this book is available
from the British Library
Gerber, Pat
Maiden voyage

ISBN 0-9519374-0-5

ACKNOWLEDGEMENTS
*Shadows Fall* first appeared in New Writing Scotland 3 (1985) then in
Northern Lights (1989), *Long Winter Sunday* appeared in New Writing
Scotland 3 (1985) and on B.B.C. Radio 4 Morning Story, an earlier
version of *To Sleep, Perchance* appeared in New Writing Scotland 4
(1986), the first version of *Swan Song Passing* appeared in Scottish
Ambassador (1986), *A Girl's Best Friend* appeared in Between the Lines
(1989), *Maiden Voyage* was runner-up in the R.N.L.I. competition
(1990), *The Seventh Wave* appeared in the Glasgow Herald (1990),
versions of *Working Mothers, School Terms* 1990 appeared in the
Glasgow Herald (1990) and in Women 2000's Meantime, and *A Hot
Flush in Winter* appeared in the Glasgow Herald (1991).

This book could not have been put together without the hard work and
encouragement of the author's husband, Cyril Gerber.

Produced by Words and Images, 2 Charlton Cottages, Speldhurst, Kent
TN3 0LH
Printed by Biddles Ltd, Walnut Tree House, Woodbridge Park,
Guildford, Surrey GU1 1DA

# CONTENTS

# STONES ON THE HILLSIDE

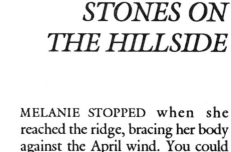

MELANIE STOPPED when she reached the ridge, bracing her body against the April wind. You could stretch your eyes up here; mountain edges piled into the distance, fans of thin blue paper. The path zig-zagged steeply to the base of the summit rock, and the other three were practically running up it. Whew – she could still keep up with them, that was for sure. She had not paused here because she was unfit but because she needed to gather her thoughts, alone for a moment, away from their constant banter. She felt a certain relief. Nothing had really changed, after all.

For some reason – probably snobbery she had to admit – she had never been up here before. Well, everyone did the old Ben. Still, the anticipation was there. No two summits were the same: you never quite knew what to expect when you got to the top of any mountain.

Look at these blokes, gambolling about. Overgrown kids. They'd fooled around on Cotopaxi too. Duncan was worse than the rest of them, though he was the oldest, and Joe and Alec were almost as bad. There was something infantile about men. The four of them had always been friends. It mustn't change now.

The sun warmed her back reassuringly, but her exhaled breath made little clouds. Of course there was no reason why their relationships should be any different – they weren't living in the dark ages any more, were they?.

'Come on Mel,' Alec was yelling. 'Thought you were going to be first at the top – what's keeping you?' Brothers.

Duncan was watching her. He looked like a wee boy when he smiled like that – vulnerable, not macho. 'We'll just do the Ben today' he had decided. Alec and Joe had moaned that they'd climbed here with every school trip since they were about twelve. But he had insisted. 'It's a Munro – might as well get it out of the way.' Their aim was to climb all the mountains over 3,000 feet by the end of the year. To her he had said 'Better take it easy, eh?'

Now he called 'Don't let them rattle you, Mel.'

The leader speaks. She had never felt him patronise her before.

She shouted back, 'I'm not rattled.' Her moment's rest had given her new wind and her boots fairly flew up the ridge path – she imagined herself in a kids' comic strip, sparks flying from the rocks in scarlet streaks. She passed the men, out of breath from their efforts. She reached the final jut of rock. Careful now. No need for roping-up on this worn old hill, but no need to be stupid either. Anyone could twist an ankle, fall, bash their head.

Boots and trusty finger-nails found their way to the top without fail. Bunch of yoiks. Flinging her arms wide she yelled at the whole world 'Done it.' And she wasn't even out of breath. The men stood below her, arms akimbo.

When Duncan reached the top he put his arms round her and nuzzled her face with his stubbly cheek. She smelled his familiar sweat. 'Ah well' he muttered into her ear, 'it may not be the Inca Trail, but it's good enough, for junior's first climb, eh? You okay, love?' And his hand was on her stomach.

Alec and Joe came up and the four of them were twirling round in a mad dance – 'Knees up Mother Brown, Knees up Mother Brown . . .'

Later, backs against a convenient rock below the summit, they got out their lunches and munched away in silence, the landscape with its famous loch laid out for their inspection below, the V-shapes of little boats sliding about on its silky surface, curving round its dark islands. Voices, high-pitched and thinned by distance, turned into a trail of brightly-clad kids crawling across the shoulder of the hill like a colourful caterpillar. Snatches of song floated upward.

'You'll tak the high road and I'll tak the low.' Was it true that the lyric had been written by a Scotsman flung into death-row at Carlisle Castle long ago? He was supposed to have written it for his lady. Had that song been all he left her with? In his day, men's lives and women's had been so different. Nowadays a girl could do anything she liked, given her health and strength, if she kept her wits about her, and if...

Whether it was the whiff of onion from Joe's sandwich or not she wasn't sure, but in a second, nausea clenched her inside, her mouth went dry, her stomach turned itself inside out and she was heaving her entire lunch into her lap.

'Oh yuck Mel, what's up with you today?' Alec leapt to his feet and moved away. He never could stand the sight of vomit.

Joe looked uncomfortable, too. 'Have you got some tissues? You usually carry half a loo-roll.' He burrowed in her pack and produced it.

Duncan helped wipe her down, but she stank of sick and her head was swimming. She stuck it between her knees, and tears of frustration ran down her cheeks.

Two years ago she and Duncan, Alec and Joe had taken a career pause – well – had given up their jobs actually. They had flown to South America to do a 2,000 mile sponsored walk down the Andes to raise money for the hospital.

Nothing in her life would ever again scare her so much, or fill her with such exhileration. When they set out she had only understood the more obvious of the risks they were running: the diseases, the guerilla bands that roamed certain areas of Ecuador and Peru, the long treks hundreds of miles from 'civilisation,' where to break an ankle could have been fatal, and where friendships would probably be tested to breaking point. Even so, she hadn't been at all sure she would survive. Undoubtedly that trip had been the highest point in her life – nothing could ever beat it.

Well, they had avoided the guerillas – or perhaps had not seemed important enough to waste bullets on. They had indeed picked up various minor diseases, the most debilitating having been the tummy bugs because vomiting and diarrhoea weakened you so, and she hated weakness. Even the blisters on your feet hardened up after the first few days.

Four people, evenly matched. The boys were six feet tall and she just on five in her socks, but that had been worked out during their trial week in the Pyrenees by adjusting the weights they carried. Carrying a maximum of forty pounds she could cover ten miles in knee-deep snow in the same time they could if handicapped with the heavy gear. Over Maram grass and moorland it was the same. They needed a medic, and she had taught herself some Quechua – the Inca's language – so she could communicate a little with the people whose land they were passing through.

Since University, she and Duncan had shared everything. They worked it out quite carefully, like most of their friends, because you didn't want to end up like your parents' generation. Marriage wasn't important, though Mum went on about 'What are you going to do when the babies come along?' She would soon find out.

The party of children had almost reached the west ridge. She got to her feet, feeling better.

'Let's escape the schoolies,' said Alec.

'Move it,' said Joe, only a few years out of school himself.

Duncan heaved to his feet and picked up Melanie's pack. 'I'll take this for you, love.'

'No.' She snatched it from him and slung it on to her shoulder. 'I can manage.'

Duncan swung away along the east ridge, Alec and Joe behind him. Mel followed, at the end of the line, ashamed of her quick temper. Would Duncan ever desert her for someone more attractive? For the first time it occurred to her that he might go off her if she didn't look sexy any more. Her own father had ditched her mother, after all, and gone off with his silly secretary – that was marriage for you. Was this new and unwelcome feeling of insecurity part of her need, however briefly, to be certain that Duncan would stick around?

The path was much narrower, less defined by erosion than the one they'd come up. From this ridge the north side of the mountain had collapsed in some primeval earthquake, leaving a dark boulder-strewn corrie. The steeply scooped southern slope was a gigantic tilting bowlful of rubble.

Traversing scree slopes always reminded her of sliding down the endless rattling pebble-banks of childhood holidays, like skating on ball-bearings, but with a safe landing-place. On scree, of course, the landing was less certain.

With a whoop, Duncan leapt off the ridge and landed in the scree, then he was bounding down it like the giant with the seven-league boots. Alec followed, rattling down the slope followed by a hail of little stones.

Joe was watching her. 'You're quiet today, Mel. Everything okay?'

No, she wanted to howl, everything's dreadful. I'm confused, I want to stay like the rest of you, not to be different, pregnant, bloody careful. But he wouldn't understand. 'I'm fine,' she said. 'On you go. I'm just coming.'

Normally she would have gone first. She watched Joe

careening downwards.

How careful was 'careful'? The first twelve weeks, the doc had said. After that you can do what you want – more or less. When she got home on Friday Duncan had whirled her round and hugged her, and promised her solemnly the baby would make no difference. They had their pact that he, being New Man, would be sharing all the responsibilities.

She didn't disbelieve him. He was a good mate, her best friend, her lover, and he meant what he said. This baby was part of their Life Plan. By Christmas it would be born. She would knock off work in November, and by this time next year she'd be back at the lab. She'd seen several of her colleages doing it. So what was the big deal? Only that she was feeling so riddled with doubts. Only that now it was too late to change her mind.

Today, for instance, they were to have climbed Nevis. Duncan had switched to this hill because it was nearer home, there wasn't a long walk in, hospitals weren't very far away. And he kept – watching her. She felt as if she were carrying a very precious piece of chrystal that belonged to him, and which he thought she might smash.

She was 'carrying' his child. The test result yesterday had been firmly positive. 'Nine weeks gone', weren't you? Gone where? The terminology of pregnancy was so familiar, from her obstetrics studies. Obstetrics – the word sounded like obstacle . . . She knew all the theory there was to know. Why then did she feel so hollow inside? Crazy thought that . . .

Alec was shouting up at her from the bottom through cupped hands, 'Come on Mel.'

'Careful,' called Duncan.

Why couldn't he stop saying that word?

Mel turned like a toddler and clambered down the short stretch of rock instead of jumping. She stood at the brink of the scree. Normally she'd have gone leaping down it like the others. Tiny yellow flowers grew between the stones, and their feathery leaves frisked round her boots.

She stepped slowly onto the dry scree-bed. Sharp stones jabbed her ankles and the ground rang as though it too were hollow, shifting, uncertain beneath her. You couldn't guess at the depth – a foot, a hundred feet? As she traversed downwards, each footfall dislodged little showers of pebbles which rolled down towards the men. Every now and then a larger one followed them.

What if she were to fall? No longer would it be simply a case of a few bruises on her person which would heal in days. All the films you ever saw about pregnant women had them falling downstairs, aborting. Suddenly a wave of guilt washed over her. She shouldn't have come today – it was selfish of her. She must not take risks – after all she knew better than most what could go wrong.

The others had given up waiting for her. Sure of her ability, they had begun to walk on down the slope. Perhaps the wash of self-pity blinded her to the loose boulder. Her boot glanced off it. In seconds it was hurtling down the mountainside, bouncing crazily, ricocheting off the rocks.

'Watch out,' she yelled, but the wind snatched her words away.

The boulder hit Joe at the back of his head. His legs crumpled beneath him.

Mel leapt down the remainder of the scree. For such a tall youth Joe made a very small heap, lying there like a rag doll someone had discarded, his green bobble hat already dark with the flood of red.

Functioning in automatic mode, Mel went through the necessary procedures and in moments had him safely on his side, his head pillowed on her backpack. He was alive, there was a pulse, and he was breathing, but he was deeply unconscious. Duncan and Alec were well down the hill by now. She shouted again, but they didn't stop.

What to do? There was no question of her carrying Joe – she hadn't the strength. He needed careful transport on a stretcher – there could be a skull fracture. She had pulled out his spare sweater, and her own, and wrapped them round him for warmth, but they had brought no survival bags today – there had seemed no need. Joe's face was ashen. She checked his pulse again, but it was steady enough.

She watched him, trying to think. This was Joe, her brother, the baby of the family. She had been too wrapped up in her own anxieties – she should have been paying attention, seen that stone, avoided it.

Voices bubbled into her consciousness, children were running, light feet clattering over the scree, their teacher calling, 'We're coming, dear – careful girls and boys, go round the *side*, I said!'

The entire school party were surrounding her, gazing down big-eyed at Joe. 'Luik at the blood, Miss,' breathed a scrub-headed boy, impressed. 'Is he deid?'

'Who's got the whistle?' she asked.

A girl in a pink anorak and white socks held it up.

'Give it a good blow then,' said the teacher.

The girl obeyed. The whistle trilled genteelly.

'Gie it tae me,' said the boy. He blew it so that it screamed down the mountainside, demanding attention. Duncan and Alec turned their heads simultaneously.

By the time they had clambered back up the slope, a make-shift stretcher had been miraculously created by the teacher out of sticks the children had brought, and a rainbow of coloured jackets and jerseys. Joe was placed tenderly in this hammock-like arrangement, bound on with belts and hair-ribbons. Duncan, Alec, the teacher, and a quarrelsome succession of the stronger pupils, carried him down the path like a wounded warrior from some long-forgotten war.

Following the procession, Mel listened to the children's chatter. They were clearly enjoying the drama. This would be a day they'd remember as surely as she would remember her day on Cotopaxi. She liked children. They were funny, and for the most part full of good intentions towards others. Women had produced these kids – women like her.

For the first time she began to think of her own child. She – or he – would be a person too, an individual. Duncan may have helped her begin this foetus, but she must build its bones, its muscle, its faculties, do all she could to ensure that it was born healthy. She must simply find a way to come to terms with the fact that Duncan could go on living on fish suppers and beer if he wanted to while she must count vitamins, minerals, refuse alcohol, rest, be careful. That Duncan would keep his trim hard body while hers would bloat and fatten into grotesque rotundity, before collapsing into the revolting jelly she had seen shaking on the front of every new mother. That, even when she had worked her stomach muscles back to fitness, she'd be left forever with splayed ribs and stretch marks.

Yet the outcome could be an adventure. She liked the unknown. This would be a challenge – something she had never tried before, a new kind of experience more physical by far than the climbing of any mere mountain, and this time she'd be going it alone. She, not Duncan, would have to go through the gates of pain to give their child life. What would it be like? What would the baby be like? What sort of a mother would she be?

The hill flattened out into birch-wood and the path broadened, easing itself down towards the car-park. Her legs were trembling, with fatigue? A waterfall splashed nearby, and she left the path for a moment, her mouth parched. Her hands tasted salty so she doubled over as if she were ducking for apples and sucked water up. Kneeling back on her heels, she rubbed cold water over her face. Did she truly want this baby? Yes.

She got up. The others were laying their burden down in the car-park.

'Miss, he's got his eyes open.' Scrub-head pointed at Joe, who was trying to sit up.

'What the hell . . . Jeez, my head.'

Duncan and Alec lifted him into the car, as gently as if

he had been a baby, explaining what had happened. He was going to be okay. The teacher dismantled the stretcher, clucking over the children as they collected their bits and pieces. There were so many children in the world, as many as the stones on the hillside.

One day, perhaps, her child would like mountains too. She put a hand on her stomach. You didn't know what to expect.

# END OF TERM

MAGGIE TURNED OVER the exam paper, her stomach full of butterflies. Scottish History – yes, she was in the right hall, yes it *was* the right paper. Now, what about the topics? Read the questions. Her watch said one-thirty, on the day of the winter solstice, in the year she'd become thirty and hope had bloomed, briefly.

She heaved a sigh, and told herself to concentrate. There was a lot to be got through on this, the last day of term. The fact that she was sitting this exam at all was a kind of protest on her part. It would count towards the degree she wouldn't stand a chance of getting, now. But at least she would have completed this, her fourth term. She shoved the seat back to make more room for her bulk and began to read through the questions.

Great – a question on ancient festivals. She'd do Yule – the death of the old year, the birth of the new. She thought for a moment, automatically releasing the cord that bound the trousers too tightly to her middle, kicking off her shoes.

All that stuff about the ancient fire festival, *and* the Romans' Saturnalia, enjoyed, so far as one could judge, till the Christians arrived, persuading folk to relinquish the old beliefs and join them, in worshipping the 'Sun of Righteousness' instead of the actual, real, lovely sun whose light gives life to everything on earth. When you thought of all the misery the Kirk, with its brutal Reformation, had brought to Scotland, the merciless medieval witch-hunts, the meanness of spirit resulting from the Reformation, the bigotry of the Orange Walks . . .

Before, folk would make great bonfires, as decoys to tempt the sun back to Scotland, for fear the days would go on getting shorter and darker till there was only eternal night.

And there was something about Shetland and Orkney – yes, the Trows or Peerie-men released from the underworld for the Merry Month of Yule to ride through the air on bulrushes till Up-Helly-aa, allowed to work mischief on folk who hadn't bothered to protect themselves by using the proper saining rites. The whiff of magic rising through the generations from a previous race of island-dwellers.

Probably a good excuse for accidental pregnancies after Yuletide parties, thought Maggie. 'Sorry Dad, it was a peerie-man.' Did pregnancy affect women's lives as much then as now? It had threatened their health, certainly, but surely a woman then hadn't cherished ambitions other than to produce a reasonable clutch of children as a gift of free workers to her husband in return for his protection?

The pressure in her pelvis discomforted her and she pushed her chair yet further back, bumping the desk of the student behind her and turning to apologise. Callum was writing already. Not yet twenty, he was just a baby to her, this bright, eccentric boy. Daily he braved the teasing of his mates for wearing his tattered kilt, working every spare minute for Scotland to have its own Assembly, debating so passionately in the Students' Union.

She was the only 'mature' student in the Department. She'd worked hard to get in – two kids to be cared for, and now no man to help, scared off last summer by finding he had a wife with the brains to argue, and who was no longer content to remain in the back-kitchen of his life.

After two years back at school, discovering she could learn, could understand, could pass Highers, she'd got into Uni. Halfway through first year she'd discovered a desire to become a politican – maybe one of the first in a Scottish Assembly. You didn't need a qualification for politics any more than you did to be a housewife, which was all she'd been till now – but she needed to achieve something to give her confidence. So here she was, reading all she could about Scottish History in an attempt to understand her own country better. She'd promised herself that, if she got her degree, she'd offer herself first for local government, then if she coped with that, she'd aim higher. Already she was a volunteer in her local constituency. But now, thanks to a parting gift from the man who had fathered her sons, she'd be grounded yet again, ambition thwarted.

Head down, she wrote on – about the fiery rites of long ago, the burnings of the Boat at Bettyhill, the Galley at Lerwick, the Clavie at Burghead, and the belief that day might never dawn again.

'It's always darkest before dawn' her best friend Angela had chirrupped yesterday. 'You'll feel different in a day or two. Christmas is coming. You're doing brilliantly at Uni, passed all your exams first go, and here you are in the middle of second year. In no time you'll have your degree, be able to go out there and get a job, get into your beloved politics. Stop worrying!'

Different in a day or two. And the real test yet to come. Maggie bent to write again, slowly at first, biting her pen top as she sought for words, then feverishly.

'Since the earliest times, the people of Scotland have celebrated the Winter Solstice. In many places wheels, balls or barrels are rolled or burned to signify the sun. For example the burning of tar-barrels at Newton Stewart and Campbeltown. The game of Yetlins at East Wemyss. At

Stonehaven they hung huge balls of inflammable material on chains or ropes, set light to them and went through the crowds swinging these around like man-made sunshine . . .'

Time passed. Maggie worked on. 'Stop writing now.' The invigilator's voice broke into her thoughts. Hurriedly finishing off her sentence, she put down the pen and read through her answers. Well, it would have to do. Pulling the trouser-cord together and knotting it again, she was conscious of the familiar heavy stone grinding against her pubic bone. She stuck her feet into her cold shoes and stood up to ease the discomfort, stretching carefully.

Callum and the others streamed away down the stone stairs in the direction of the Unions, but Maggie didn't follow. Instead, she left the exam hall head down, not feeling sociable. Usually, after an exam, she'd commiserate with the others, go for a comforting pint before heading homeward but today she felt drained, exhausted, nervous.

Giving herself time to redirect her thoughts, she plodded through the archway to the south-facing terrace beyond the quadrangle. The sun looked blearily across at her through chiffon clouds as though it was too tired to bother heaving itself up in the sky any longer. She knew how it felt. No wonder the early Scots had thought it needed tempting, to stay with them.

She loved this view, out across the raw meat-red of Kelvingrove Gallery and the bland back of the Transport Museum to Yorkhill, with its tall black childbirth factory. It was a kind of descending view of humanity, from Learning, to Art, to Engineering, to the blood and guts of procreation. Or was it an *as*cending view? Should we perhaps have a higher regard for the physical facts of life than we do? Maggie allowed herself the luxury of waiting till the sun finally sank behind the Gleniffer Braes, and the day died. There was no need to hurry.

The rusty hatchback started with a sniffle and a cough, headlamps fingering the darkness. It would be a short journey. She wouldn't go home – she'd said goodbye to the kids before school this morning. They'd have gone to Angela's after school, to stay for a day or two till her return. She'd go shopping to kill time.

The chemist was crammed with people trying to fight off winter ills so they could keep working, buying last minute Christmas presents. Talc for aged aunts, aftershave for lovers – would she ever have another lover, would she ever *want* one, to disrupt her life yet again, create havoc with her uncertain emotions?

Treat yourself to something really nice,' Angela had said, so she bought one of these pretty baskets of matching soap, body lotion and scent. Pale yellow, scented with primroses, to make her think of Springtime. Squeezing through the crowd, she paid and left.

Butterflies again. The hospital car park in darkness, and a slow drizzle of rain. It made a halo round the dim blue light that indicated Reception. There could be no turning back now, no thoughts of any kind would help her through the next ordeal. This time the test would be utterly physical.

The hospital smell, the undressing, the sense of rising excitement alongside crawling dread. The tight cuff of the blood-pressure meter, polite chit-chat of the nurse while dainty fingers shave off every vestige of pubic hair. The feeling of being a sacrificial animal undergoing preparation for some strange human ritual.

Then suddenly the cramps come. Radiating through her lower back first, rolling through her pelvic floor, not painful yet. Familiar as any hard-working muscles, the pull increases, tightening, like teenage period pains, like back-ache after a day's digging in the old garden.

Maggie smiles, ironically, at the nurse. Her time has come – and at such an inconvenient hour, too. The hospital had scheduled her for the production line tomorrow morning, with the ceremonial breaking of the waters, the chemical injection to induce contractions, the computer attached to the appropriate parts to monitor progress – and here she is labouring away already, fit to bust, and most of the nurses and doctors off-duty for the night. The nurse shrugs. A scared-looking junior feels Maggie's belly with cold hands. The newly-qualified doctor – probably doing her second night on call after a day's work – listens vaguely to the foetal heart. Is the baby in distress?

'Take it gently now dear, gently. Do your breathing.'

As if she'd stop. 'I'll huff and I'll puff and I'll blow your house down.' Count – do anything to distract yourself from the increasing need to push. Think of today's exam – burning Clavies, oh the Stonehaven fireball is burning me, burning me, searing wounds in my flesh. The sun of last Spring that day your seed was planted, last act of your deserting father. Will I ever see another sunrise? Will I, this time, split open and die? Think positively – about the baby, he/she's a person too – why do we have to be born through suffering? To give us a preview of the life to come – to come – to come –

Gas and air hiss, dulling consciousness, sweeping her into pastures green, a loch rolling away to the south, the sun rising over hills, the first primrose growing at her feet, bending to pick it, crouching, pushing -

'Wait, Mrs MacAlpine, wait. We're just going to help you on to the trolley . . . off to theatre . . forceps . . . soon be over.'

Back arching as muscles contract again. Wheeling along the corridor, lights streaming overhead. Huh, huh.

'Theatre, dear.'

A daze of lights, men in green masks – green men – Peerie men? They lift the sheet, gaze between her spreadeagled legs, discuss her. The hard stone to be expelled, so – huh, huh, – slowly. Wanting to – *having* to push and *push*, ripe as a peapod, ready to deliver. Lie back sweating. Another one coming – more gas and air – O.K. now dear, give it all you've got right down the back.

*Pu-u-ush* – and the stone is out.

'Well done, dear.' The nurse smiles.

Long slow grunting heave. Red meat-ball head – so beautiful. A scribbling of black hair. Plump little barrel-body streaked with blood and mucus – a girl to share her woman's life. All fingers and toes correct. Dark, finely-drawn eyebrows.

People are clapping, laughing. Who – ? She looks up. A crowd of young people in green clothes, looking down at her. The doctor explains – students. It's the end of term, and this the first non-induced birth they've ever actually witnessed. They'd been called in for the occasion, from parties, carol-singing, Daft Friday. It'll be so useful for their degree exams. What's the baby's name? Hope? How unusual!

Midnight strikes on the University bell across the Kelvin. On a wave of post-natal euphoria, Hope warm and quiet on her breast, Maggie speaks. 'Yes, I have decided to go on with my course. If necessary I'll take her in to lectures. I'll try, anyway. I'll work to get a creche set up, for other mothers who want to study. I must finish, for her sake, must work to make a better Scotland for her generation of girls to grow up into.'

She sat up. The students looked on, encouragingly. 'But even if I don't succeed, the sun will continue to rise. It will remain longer in the sky tomorrow, and the Spring will come.' Even to herself, Maggie sounded like a politician.

# *MUMMY*

ANNABEL FOLLOWED her mother backwards through time. After the computer spat out their tickets in the museum foyer they drifted down forty centuries, slowly at first via World War Two, Fashions of the Twenties and Thirties, The Great War, Victoriana, then taking a quantum leap to the Romans.

A sleepy security man checked their tickets. 'You're a pair of early birds. Not usually anyone here till later.'

'We have a lot to get through today,' her mother said.

Passing into the beginnings of pre-history, Annabel lingered in the Celtic Period. Here there would be peace to discuss her UCCA form with Mum. She liked the chunky Celtic jewellery. The gleaming silver and bronze torques, necklets and armbands must have lain untouched for years in their protective glass shell.

Her mother was moving past the far side of the showcase, which distorted and magnified the embarrassing bulge of her thickened torso. She looked grotesque.

What did it feel like to have a baby squirming about inside you? Annabel knew it squirmed because one day her mother had said, 'Here, put your hand on my tummy and feel the baby,' and she had felt this monstrous wriggling thing beneath the skin. Her mother's pregnancy horrified and sickened Annabel, though she'd die rather than admit it. You were supposed to be pleased. She shuddered, remembering how hard it had been to tell Maeve.

She and Maeve often discussed sex, sometimes seriously, other times having a giggle, though neither of them had actually gone the whole way with Johnny or Allan yet. Maeve's ma was always going on about teenage pregnancy, and issuing Dire Warnings. She was a social worker and saw a lot of girls 'in trouble'. Maeve's ma had had her tubes cut. What was it like to have your tubes cut?

'Annabel, come and look. This is your kind of thing.' Mum had lumbered on into 'Ancient Egypt'. 'They've opened the mummy, Shepenhor. Last time I was here she was all sealed up.'

A thin layer of dust muted the creamy pastel colours on the curved lid of the coffin, but you could make out the design: the full-length portrait of a woman with sweeping dark eyes and long black hair cut square like Cleopatra's, wearing an ankle- length dress covered with dozens of little pictures like comic strips, outlined in black and painted terracotta pink or Prussian blue. What did they mean?

The lid was like the outer shell of one of those Russian dolls that have smaller dolls inside each other, made of thin curved wood. It was propped up on wires so you could see inside. A long bundle of greyish cloth, frayed at the edges, lay there. Dust to dust, ashes to ashes. Annabel shivered. 'That's creepy. But surely they wouldn't leave an actual – ' She'd never seen a dead body, well you never really got the chance, did you? When grandfather had died, she'd asked if she could see him – she'd only been ten then – but various grown-ups had been shocked, had said it 'wasn't suitable.'

Her mother peered in. 'Isn't she tiny? Of course, you can't tell whether it's a she or a he, can you, under all that wrapping? I wonder if it's a child?'

Annabel suddenly recognised a shrivelled toe among the

raggy ends. Horrified, she slid sideways to read the information notice. A life-sized X-Ray print was pinned to the wall, bearing the legend 'A young woman. This is the height she would have stood. The texts on the lid are prayers to gods and goddesses that they should protect her in the Afterlife.' 'Gosh.' She stood beside it. 'She *was* small.'

'Yes,' her mother breathed. 'Poor kid. I wonder what her life was like, what she died of so young. Look, it says her father was In-Amun-nif-nebu, and her mother's name was Irt-irw. How on earth do they know that?'

'And she lived in 700 B.C.' Keep reading the notice, so you didn't have to look at these dreadful toes again. The blotchy picture showed little feet, and leg bones dangling. The backbone and rib-cage were exactly like an X-Ray Annabel had seen of herself once. But the skull looked squashed. It grinned lop-sidedly at her, and she found herself fraught with thoughts of restless spirits, and horror videos. 'How do they know it's a female?' she asked, to keep her mind on realities.

'It's the pelvis, I think. They can tell by its shape – wider than a man's, to contain the –'

'What's this?' Annabel's finger traced a darker whorl in the shadows of the pelvic bones.

'Could it be – the skeleton of a baby, do you think?' Her mother put an arm round her, gazing at the photograph enthralled. 'Look, isn't that a little backbone, all curled over like a little shrimp – and there's the head?'

'It's just a shadow on the X-Ray, Mother.' Annabel didn't mean to sound so cross. Why did her mother irritate her so?

She was still drooling over the thing; 'The picture's so faint. I'd never have noticed. Maybe you should do Archaeology after all, Annabel. Our baby is about that size, now. I saw it on the scan yesterday. Poor little mite, and all these thousands of years ago.'

Annabel kept her eyes on the X-Ray, not wanting to see again the dreadful bundle in the box. 'Mum, nobody *dies* when they're having babies now, do they?'

'No, of course not.' Then her mother's posture changed subtly, as though she had made a decision. 'Well, actually of course, dear, it is *possible*. But only if something goes drastically wrong. It's all a great deal safer than ever before.' She took a deep breath. 'Annabel, I've never really asked how you feel about this baby. I did decide to tell you early on so you'd have time to get used to the idea, but I suppose it must have come as a bit of a shock.'

Caught by surprise, her defences down, Annabel found herself hissing 'A shock? Mother, you must be joking. It's disgusting, at your age.' The words were tumbling out of her mouth, she couldn't stop them. 'What if *I* wanted a baby? In a primitive society I'd probably have *two* by now. *You*'d only be fit to be a toothless old granny.' Her mother looked stricken. Annabel's tongue had taken on a life of its own, careening away out of control, beyond her brain. 'It's been awful. When you threw up that morning at the school gates, in front of *everyone*. My shoes were splashed with sick all day, you made me *smell*. And now you're so – so fat. You haven't come to a single thing at school since – since Dad *did* it to you. And – and how do you think I'll be able to work for my exams? They really matter to me, you know. If I don't pass then I'll end up on the scrap heap like you, only capable of – of procreation . . .'

'Annabel, I'd no idea you felt – '

Half of Annabel wanted to run away. Last year she would have rushed out of the room and slammed the door behind her. Now she stood her ground. 'And what if it's handicapped?' She glared down at her mother. 'Did either of you stop to think about that? Don't you read the papers? Haven't you *heard* that women over forty give birth to – to freaks?' She stuffed her fist into her trembling mouth to stop the torrent of hateful words, horrified at what she'd done, tears of anger and guilt streaming down her face.

Her mother's physical presence seemed to sink down and

away from her, to diminish in stature as though her very bones had shrunk. Till this moment she had been in charge, had so kindly brought Annabel here to make her fateful decision; should she opt for her passion, Medieval Archaeology, or for something sensible that would guarantee her a job, like Computer Studies. All of a sudden she became just another human being, full of doubts and fears just like herself. Why didn't she say something – fight back?

A dull flush had risen over her mother's face and neck. 'It's different for you, Annabel. All you young people seem to care about is your careers. I never had a proper job. Just recently I'd been planning to do some training, like Maeve's mum, once you'd left home.'

'She's sensible. Don't you and Dad do contraception?' Annabel couldn't believe what she was saying to her mother, talking to her now as frankly as she did to Maeve, almost as if they were – sisters.

'Accidents happen.'

'Abortion is legal here.'

'I – couldn't bear the thought of it.'

'But it's a perfectly simple operation.'

'Nothing is that simple, Annabel. After I had you, I lost – I had three miscarriages, couldn't seem to hang onto the little souls. For some reason, this one stuck.' She put her hand on her stomach.

'I don't remember anything like that.' Annabel felt as if a bucketful of cold water had been thrown over her anger, but kept her voice high. There was some sort of underground conflict going on here between them, though she couldn't work it out. She knew she had to keep on top.

Her mother sat down on a bench, heaved her bag on to her lap and drooped over it. 'When you were little, Dad and I wanted you to have at least one brother or sister.'

'Isn't it a bit late, now?' Annabel was struggling to stay in charge.

'Yes. But – doesn't this baby deserve as much chance to

live as you do?'

'Oh I don't care.' Annabel's burst of power was ebbing away into doubt and uncertainty. She sounded, to herself, like a disgruntled child. 'Well, you needn't expect any help from me. That's all.'

Her mother was straightening her backbone again. She stood up, smiling. 'You'll feel differently when you see the baby, dear. Now come on, let's go and have a coffee and discuss *your* future. That's what matters today.'

Annabel's voice went very quiet. 'See Mum, part of me *does* want to study, try for a degree, and all that. But – I look in prams, you know? Am I weird or what? None of the others do that.'

'No, dear, not weird. But surely you want to have a more – interesting life than I had?' She ruffled Annabel's hair. 'Silly girl. You're quite normal. Join the club: you want children *and* a career. It's just that maybe it's easier if you organise the career first.' She turned back towards the mummy. 'This Egyptian lass. In her day women were wives – or whores. Now it's different. You can't map out your entire life in one day. All you can do is decide on the first step. I just don't want you to make – the same mistakes I did. And there's plenty of time for babies – look at me!'

Annabel looked at her. This mother of hers was as frail and riddled with uncertainties as she herself. She couldn't really tell Annabel – anything.

'I'll never have a career, now. But they say a late baby keeps you young, at least.' The voice trailed off again.

Already this baby was pushing Annabel out of her cosy nest. It looked as though she would have to fly, somehow, on her own. The thought of independence was suddenly exciting. Would she manage, away at university? Would she be able to make friends, force herself to work, feed and clothe herself, manage her grant, cope with missing Allan, doing without the friendship of Maeve? She must train herself not to be so fearful, so full of doubt. She'd begin now. Bending low, she peered into the mummy's box. Dusty bandages swaddled the slight figure of the aristocratic girl who had died of pregnancy with no other chance of life, constricted by a culture that turned women into ornamental prize cattle.

The body no longer frightened her. Rather, it seemed to Annabel, it was a figure of pathos, so small, so unfulfilled, so – decorated. How fettered the whole history of women had been by their physical frailty, the bondage of their dependence. Things were better now – she'd be crazy not to take advantage of that.

'Come on, Mum. Let's go. Listen. I'll *do* the History course. I mean, computers? Technology just does what it's told. I'd rather know more about what happens to people's dreams, where their ideas came from, why they did what they did, how they coped.' Annabel began to lead the way back up through the centuries towards The Celtic Period. 'It's so complicated, being female. Everything fits inside everything else, like a Russian doll. What I decide now will affect me and you, and Allan, *and* my kids – one day. Won't it?'

'Yes, dear.' Her mother trudged heavily behind her through to The Present Day where she asked the security man where the coffee shop was. 'Oh boy, do I need a seat.'

But the security man didn't hear her. He was fast asleep on his chair.

She sighed, and as she squeezed through the swing doors Annabel saw that she was melon-shaped, more interesting than ugly.

They linked arms with each other and made for the stairs.

# THE PARTY

WHEN CHILDREN about to be thirteen request birthday parties, mothers experience a variety of emotions – including stark terror. Distracted, harrassed, just in from work, I had stupidly said 'yes dear' to the wrong question and here we were, the doorbell ringing.

This party, Annie promised, would be different.

'O.K.' I eyed my daughter, feeling the ground slip from beneath me. 'Convince me. How – different?'

'A dinner party. Like you have.'

'Pardon?' Surprise is definitely the best form of attack. I was lost for words, including 'NO'. There is something about this child's line of attack that disables my thought- processes.

How sweetly she had pressed home her advantage, promised to do all the cooking.

'What will you give them?'

I ought to have known. She had it all planned. My shorthand notebook was whipped from behind her back and the lists read out. 'Corn-on-the cob, chicken and chips, trifle. And it's all to be blue.'

'Blue?'

'Napkins and things. Blue candles in these old bottles.'

'Old bottles? And the clearing up?' The defeat sounds in my voice.

'I'll do it ALL, the hoovering, the washing-up.' As if she is giving me the greatest present in the world. Patting the dog she said 'Lulu will help.'

I could make jokes about being nuts to allow another party after the last fiasco, and crackers as a result. I don't like being a social pariah. I don't like being ostracised by the entire gateful of mums with whom, every half-day, I have to queue up for my quota of the school run. But I'm too tired.

The doorbell rings again.

I open it to Mrs Fanshawe, who ushers in Sophie demure in pink leggings and cream lace.

There are six of them altogether, including that child Bernadette in skin-tight black with matching lipstick.

'Bernadette's mum and dad go out when she's having a party. Why don't you and Dad go to the flicks or something?'

I won that round.

While Annie entertains her guests to passion-fruit cocktails (blue) in the lounge I inspect her table. The blue linen tablecloth (my best), is set with blue and white china (my wedding present from Mother-in-law), the best silver, blue napkins (hand-embroidered, starched and murder to iron), and blue candles have been stuffed into my antique glass bottles.

The actual dinner goes very well. One of Annie's good points (she has approximately three in all) is that she likes cooking. I delegate the evening meal to her once a week – it channels her energies. Apart from cooking, she's fairly disreputable really, though lovable.

The deal Annie and I have made is that, after the dinner, they'll watch a video, then play board games and cards quietly till the parents collect.

I serve coffee in little cups, as arranged.

The video they have selected, from all the rich variety available, is not *Manon des Sources*. It is *The Texas Chain Saw*

*Massacre*. Have you seen it? Neither had I. After fifteen minutes I remove it and cut the plug off the TV power flex.

For a time all is quiet. I encouraged Donald to do that bit of extra work at the office tonight, feeling I could handle this better on my own. I knit in the bedroom listening to Bach on the radio. Gradually I relax. Maybe this party has been rather a good idea, just a few girls together.

At around eight p.m. there comes a shriek. I sit bolt upright. What on earth is going on? When the screams reach neighbour- annoyance potential I burst into the party room. It is in pitch darkness.

A body flings itself into my arms yelling 'Save me, Annie's Mum.' It is Sophie, her long hair all over the place, her eyes on stalks.

'What is going on?' My school-marm voice. Automatically clutching the child, I am haunted by memories of seventies student parties.

'Murder In The Dark, Mum.' Annie appears out of the gloom. 'Want to play?'

'Something quieter, now, if you please, girls. The Monopoly's in the bottom drawer.' I help myself to a pack of cards.

Back in my bedroom, I try Patience.

For a while there is peace. Lulu barks, and there are feet running all over the house, more shrieks, and Lulu is giving an operatic performance of woofings.

Annie appears. 'Mum, Lulu has eaten the Monopoly.'

The house is a snowstorm of paper money, and on the floor are the crumbs that remain from the board along with three half- chewed hotels.

'She's swallowed ALL the houses.'

Catching a flying £1,000 pound note and picking £5.0 out of Sophie's ponytail, I lay down the law. Only half an hour to go till collecting time. Something peaceful, PLEASE girls.

I try a book next and, deep in *The Feminist Backlash*, I am soon vaguely conscious that the voices have dropped to tolerable levels next door. It takes me longer to notice that the sounds have stopped altogether.

When the unnatural silence impinges on my consciousness, I decide they must be playing cards – something quiet that requires concentration. They are really a good little crowd. Gratefully I sink once again into the mental challenges of *Backlash*, till I am distracted again by the ringing of the bell.

Ah, it must be the first parent. A crescendo of giggling rises from the next room, but nobody is going to the door.

Wearily, not feeling like an in-depth discussion on My Interpretation of the latest School testing system, I get to my feet. Thank goodness birthdays only turn up once a year. Maybe soon Annie will be too old for parties? I was too slow. Our hostess beat me to it. Unfortunately.

As I reached the hallway everything went into slow motion. Annie, looking somewhat dishevelled, minus her shirt, flung the front door wide. Sophie's mum stood there, smiling.

'Whew!' gasped Annie. 'You've JUST saved Sophie from losing her knickers!'

Parental eyebrows shoot skywards. Eyeballs swivel beyond Annie, past me standing transfixed beneath the chandelier. The entire street can see inside my house.

Clothing litters the floor. Bernadette streaks past stark naked, squeaking 'Cripes,' chased by Sophie in her knickers.

Still trying to hang on to formality, Sophie's mum utters faintly, 'Dressing-up? How nice. But aren't you girls a little beyond– ?'

'No no,' cries Annie. 'Cards. Bernadette's won. We've been playing strip-poker.'

# *A DOG'S LIFE*

THE MARCH
NIGHT was cold.
The stars looked
very far away in the black sky, the moon hanging like a curved
knife over the skeleton trees. Somewhere in the distance a
dog howled a long, miserable howl. Jane stood in the porch,
looking down the curve of the drive into the night. Where
could she go, now?

Seconds ago she'd slammed the door on her childhood.
Even now she realised that the quarrel had been stupid, over
nothing. But suddenly she'd had enough, she was leaving,
getting out. She'd stamped out before, after quarrels of one
sort or another, but this time it was be for real. This time
she'd show them. Sixteen-year-olds could do as they pleased,
couldn't they – leave school, join the army, have sex?
Sixteen-year-olds were old enough to stand on their own feet
– they didn't need bloody parents telling them what to do all
the time. It was a dog's life.

She'd think of something.

Head high – they might be watching her – she stalked
down the three broad steps and set off fast down the drive.
She kept up the pace till she was round the bend by the
rhododendron bushes and out of sight of the windows. By

the time she reached the gates she was dragging her feet through the gravel. She crossed the road to the bus shelter. It was cold. She glanced at her watch – surely the last bus couldn't have gone yet?

As she waited, she could just see the top storey of the house that had been her home for as long as she could remember. One by one the lights went out, till the whole house disappeared, as black as the surrounding trees. Silence surrounded her and her brain was numb.

Some time later the sound of an engine focused her attention. Headlights wobbled into view.

The ancient bus roared past on its way to its turning stop. In five minutes it would be back. Jane felt in her bag for her transcard. It was there all right. So, she'd travel into town – it was only five miles or so, maybe meet up with some people. She liked the older crowd and it was only eleven o'clock, so most of them would still be out, even though it was Monday night. Older folk were out every night, going to the various nightclubs and such. They'd let her go with them, even if she was a bit under-age. She knew she looked eighteen. She could pay them back tomorrow for the ticket and any drinks, use her cash-card.

The bus was warm inside, and bright. It smelt of old coats and cigarette smoke. The driver looked at her curiously as she showed her school pass, but said nothing. There was nobody else. Once ensconced on the top deck she examined the contents of her bag. She'd tipped it out on her bedroom floor in her hurry, and stuffed in whatever she could lay her hands on, grabbed her jacket, hurled a final insult at her father and run out.

There was her bank card thank goodness, two pairs of knickers – clean, her book from the school library, her address book, a jersey, some make-up and a Twix bar.

The centre of town wasn't quite as busy as she had imagined. As midnight clanged on the old clock, several of the shop-window lights went out. Where would all her friends be – where could she start looking? Oh well, perhaps she could talk her way into one of the clubs. It would be like acting in the school play – if she convinced herself she was eighteen, she'd be able to convince others.

The burly bouncer outside Trasky's laughed in her face. 'Away home to yer maw,' he said. 'Lassies your age shouldnae be tryin' to get in here. D'ye want us to lose wir licence?'

She tried up at Screamers but they wouldn't let her in either. 'Ticket holders only, and Monday's the over-thirties night anyway dear.'

Chilled to the bone, needing the loo, Jane wandered into the railway station. The Ladies' was locked and in darkness. The clock said one-thirty. She sat on an orange plastic seat. Other seats were occupied too. An old man lay opposite her, a stream of liquid trickling from his damp trousers into a pool of yellow, a bottle hanging out of his pocket and his grey stubbled face slack with sleep.

A thin boy not much older than herself came and sat beside her. His straggly hair had been dyed puce and pale blue, his trainers were filthy and his jeans split across both knees and frayed at the bottoms. His face was greenish pale and he had black shadows around his eyes that made him look like a vulture. He moved closer so that he pressed against her. He smelt. She edged away. He followed.

'Waiting for a train?' he enquired.

Jane didn't respond.

'Got anything to eat?'

'Fuck off,' she said.

'Oh oh, nasty language, and me thinking you looked a posh bit. Give us a quid then.'

'Leave me alone.' Jane edged away again.

'C'mon, give us a quid and I'll go.' His hand felt for her pocket.

Jane tore herself free. 'I'm – I'm going for the late bus. I'll not bother waiting on the the train. There's no peace in this station.'

'No, stay. I'll not annoy you. Oh-oh, look who's doin' the rounds.'

A tall young policeman stood looking down at them. 'You can't spend the night here, you two. Off you go now.'

He thought *she* was like this scruffy boy? Couldn't he see she was – different?

The youth got up and pulled her to her feet, putting an arm round her. 'Come on, hen. There's nae room at the inn – and he's got nothin' better tae do than harrass folks like us. I've got a train tae catch.'

She pulled herself away from him. 'I'm not – '

The policeman said, 'That's right, on yer bikes the pair of you,' and watched as they walked down the empty platform from which the London trains usually left.

Stopping at another seat, sitting down, the boy said I'm for London you know.'

'London?'

'Uh huh. The big time. Find myself a group – I do vocals – ye can make a fortune down there. That's where it's all happening. Can't get work up here, only pickin' up other folk's rubbish and that. Scotland is dead.'

'Oh yes, very likely.'

'I was lead-singer, with the school group.'

'When was that? In the stone age?'

'You're hard, you know that? When you come in just now, I thought you looked nice.' He spat. 'You're just a hard wee bitch like all the others.'

Jane had argued enough for one night. This was not what she'd left home for. 'Get lost,' she said, and got up. Something she saw in his eyes made her say more gently, 'I'll look out for you in the charts. See you,' before trailing out of the station into the orange fog.

The queue for the late bus stood in the square, bright with laughter and chat. People's breath puffed clouds of steam as they spoke to each other. Hot air, Jane thought, looking for any familiar faces. She found nobody.

Too tired to think, she wandered down an alleyway and squatted to pee, unable to wait any longer. As she rose, pulling up her jeans, she noticed a dog rustling among some papers further along the road. It had found a half-eaten bag of chips and, looking over its shoulder to see if there was any competition to be fought off, it picked the bag up delicately in its mouth and trotted towards her.

Jane loved dogs. That was another thing they'd never allowed her at home. Every Christmas the hope had risen in her mind that *this* year they'd give her a puppy – they knew it was what she wanted more than anything – and every year she'd had to feign gratitude for a doll's pram, a skateboard, a new coat, a bicycle.

She gave a low whistle. The dog came towards her, wagging its tail. Its ears were cocked and its eyes were bright and sort of cheeky – it looked so funny. She laughed. 'Come on,' she said 'Fetch it here.'

It came right up to her and dropped the package by her feet, waiting politely, it seemed, for her to do something. She stroked its head. Its fur was stiff and matted. She picked up a cold chip and offered it to the dog. Looking up at her, it took the chip gently from her. Then it was eating voraciously. Running her hand down its back, she could feel each knobble of its backbone, each rib beneath the scraggy skin. It must be half-starved, poor dog.

She wandered back towards the brightly-lit square. The dog followed at her heels. She stood in the bus queue. It lay down at her feet chewing the greasy paper bag left over from the chips with relish. He was one of the oddest-looking dogs Jane had ever seen. Basically black, his head was rough and hairy like a terrier's, his body hairy too but shaped like a greyhound's, and his legs incredibly long and thin. He had a white bib like a collie's, though it was rather grimy.

The bus arrived at the stop. In the rush of getting on, Jane forgot about the dog. Her purse, her pass and her bank-card with it, had gone. Somehow, she must have dropped them out of her bag. The few coins she managed to scrape together from the bottom of her pockets amounted to just enough to take her to the edge of the town, no further. She pushed her way to the back of the bus and sat down, weary to her bones. And then the dog was pushing his snout into her hand. He must have followed her. He laid his head on her lap and gazed soulfully up at her. She dozed.

One by one the laughing couples left the bus, their arms entwined, till no-one was left but Jane and the dog.

'You're out late kid,' said the driver as she got off at the last stop. 'Your mum know where you are?'

No, thought Jane, pulling her collar up round her ears. And if she did she probably wouldn't care.

The diesel fumes lingered in the frosty air long after the bus had turned back towards the town. The dog pattered after her along the road. Where were they going now? She sat for a while on a wall, remembered her Twix bar, got it out and gave one piece to the dog. 'What's your name?'

He munched, his head low, teeth glued together with the toffee.

'No, you can't tell me, can you? How about 'Stranger'? I roll up at the house and tell Mum and Dad I've brought a little Stranger home with me – ' she burst into hysterical giggles, which became sobs, and then she was crying her heart out, her face buried in the dog's smelly coat.

Eventually she ran out of tears. The dog licked her face, his tongue rough and warm, his breath still smelling of vinegar from the chips. Her feet were freezing and her legs stiff with cold when she got up.

'Can't stay here, Stranger' she said, feeling it was nice to have someone to talk to. 'Better start walking. Come on. It's at least three miles yet.'

Once her eyes were accustomed to the dark, she could see surprisingly well. The moon was up, and though only a sliver, its pale silvery light picked out the road ahead quite clearly, except where it dived into the shadows of a wood.

You could see the outlines of hills and trees and the distant mountains, and the texture of some of the fields. An owl screeched and she nearly jumped out of her skin, feeling exposed in the moonlight. In the darkness of the wood she was hardly scared at all, feeling protected, with Stranger at her heel. Beyond the wood lay farm-land and pasture. Corduroy ribs of plough were striped with ice and in every hollow lay folds of mist. The air smelled sharp now, and clean. Blisters were hurting the toes of her left foot and the muscles of her thighs felt as though they would burst with weariness. Left, right, left, right. She wouldn't think yet about home.

The youth in the station came back into her mind. Was he on the London train yet? He didn't look as if he could afford the fare. Did he have the talent to make it in music? How could you tell if you had any ability? How did you know if you could stand on your own two feet? She remembered her purse, but quelled the thought he might have pinched it from her. Surely she would have felt something? Well, if he had taken her money, he might be able to get to London after all – which was what he really wanted out of life.

For herself – what was it that she wanted? A dog? There was no shortage of money – she could get another cash-card, and there would be plenty in her account. Was she just a spoiled bitch – like that boy had said? And, if you were spoiled, how did you un-spoil yourself? How could you get to be good? And what on earth could she get to be good at – good enough to make her own living, to be independent of parents for ever?

The short-cut across the estate led from a padlocked gate. She clambered over it and called to the dog. He tried to jump it, but lacked the strength. Three times he attempted it, only to batter himself against the it. The fence was for sheep, all little squares, so he couldn't get through that. What to do? She couldn't face the long way round. Back over the gate. Pick Stranger up. Heave him over. Then up and over it again herself.

She found the path through the grounds easily enough – she had escaped this way before. Green mounds of moss edged it like little cushions, and Stranger made forays amongst the ferns, but always returned to her. As she neared the house she began to wonder what to do with him.

'The garden shed – will you be happy there Stranger? Or won't you like being shut in?' Oh the ignominy that was facing her, the business of saying 'I'm back' and eating humble pie, again. The lectures from Father 'when I was your age . . .' and from Mum 'I couldn't sleep for worrying – you've caused me so much anxiety, why can't you be like other girls . . .' How could she take any more of it? And yet what could she do, out here in the cold where there was nowhere to go for the rest of her life? Could she go to London like that boy in the station? No chance – he was in cloud cuckoo land, wasn't he – she didn't have the talent to be in any school group either. The only thing she could do was biology.

The garden shed smelt of straw and tar, so familiar, so *homey*. It felt less cold in there. Father always kept it tidy – 'a place for everything, and everything in its place' – and saw to it that the gardener did too. Even in the dark she knew where each item would be.

The dog's stomach gave a long rumble.

'Oh, poor Stranger. There's nothing more to eat tonight – but there'll be plenty in the morning. Bacon, sausages, toast –' her mouth began to water. 'You could – er – help yourself to water from the lily pond if you're thirsty.' She took him across the silent lawn, and cupped her palms for some of the peaty liquid herself.

'I know, Stranger. We'll both spend the rest of the night in the hut. That way you won't think I've deserted you. You won't be lonely, like that boy. Anyway, if I tried to get into the house I'd set off all the alarms. *They* might as well have a bit more worry. Might soften them up in the morning, when I introduce *you*, my friend, might make them behave better in future, if they think I really did run away for ever.' She shared out the pile of sacks, some for herself, some for the dog. She yawned. 'As if I'd be so immature. Maybe I should be a vet.'

The dog stalked round and round on his pile of sacks, then, sighing, curled up with his back warm against hers.

She tucked her sacks around her and fell asleep.

# *TO SLEEP, PERCHANCE*

'AND THEY ALL LIVED happily ever after.' Meg closed the book and sighed. Why did she go on telling these lies to her daughter after what had happened to her, to them both? Her mouth uttered the words, but her mind had frozen into slow-action replay.

'One more, Mummy?' the child's eyes held hers. 'Tell me Daddy's one.'

Two hours had passed since 'Daddy' had left. Although Lisa would soon be going to school she still liked being read to and the old fairy-tales, which she knew almost by heart, were her favourites. Till last night it had been the norm for Meg and 'Daddy' to read one story each before tucking her up for the night – a little routine to give the child a feeling of security to help her sleep peacefully. 'Sorry love. I've got to prepare for tomorrow's classes.' Apologising, always inadequate to meet the demands made on her by others. Weakening – perhaps tonight extra pains were needed – 'Well, which is it to be?'

'The Sleeping Beauty. Because of going to the ballet tomorrow.'

The book was old and grey, the paper rough-edged, flannel-thick. They'd found it in a junk-shop in Penzance, long before Lisa had been born. Page forty – Meg's age. Life was supposed to begin now, not end. The illustrations were like misty memories of past pantomimes, of dreams. Pink, blue and brown courtiers followed a golden coach through autumn trees, the caption: 'All the company returned to the Royal Palace to find a great feast arranged.' Like their wedding, the billowing white dress that had lied about her purity, the stiffly formal hotel meal, the sense of escape afterwards.

Lisa had turned to the next picture. Rose-brown, sage-green, the princess asleep with two cherubs skipping through a cloud of golden mist and the prince looking at her, his hand on his heart. 'He beheld the loveliest vision he had ever seen.' 'Daddy' had once called Meg his princess, in these distant days when she had believed you really did live happily ever after.

'Read, Mummy.' Lisa knew the ritual. First the pictures, then the story, then the goodnight kiss. So little to make the child feel safe and loved.

'Once upon a time there lived a King and a Queen, who lacked but one thing on earth to make them entirely happy.' She knew how they'd felt. Married twelve years and his parents always on at you about the joys of a family. They never thought about the problems, the responsibilities, but she had stuck to her principles. Until they could do without her salary she'd stay on the Pill. Later, as she realised he was becoming bored with her, she had given in. Perhaps a child would indeed bring them together again, a son to carry on his family name, a sop to tradition. But after barren years of tests and trials she had given up, deciding after all to make her mark through work. Just after she had won her first big promotion, she had begun to feel sick in the mornings. It had not been some life-threatening disease, it had turned out to be Lisa, and at the age of thirty-five Meg had had to rethink her life for the first time.

He had gone off her pregnant body. Later, disappointed

that she failed to bring forth a son, he had been slow to accept Lisa and Meg had started calling him 'Daddy' to convince him of his role, to make him feel a part of things. She had gone back to work, freed by the au pair girls till 'Daddy' of the increasing paunch and the roving eye had made life impossible for them and, one after the other, they had left in disgust. Now Lisa went to a childminder like the children of other lecturers.

Meg dragged her mind back to the task in hand. 'They invited all the fairies they could find in the land to be godmothers to the Princess Aurora.'

'Tell me about my christening, Mummy.' Anything to keep her there.

Meg shook her head. 'Not tonight, darling.' But as she read mechanically on, Lisa's baptism drifted into her mind. Even then he had been chasing one of her friends. Why had it always been someone she knew? Of course if there were others she'd not have found out. As it was, someone always felt the need to inform her, usually after the affair was over, for her own good. Her friends would tell her of the times he had made passes at them and then they'd all laugh together at his stupidity, his arrogance in thinking they'd risk their friendship with her for his favours. One especially, Zilla, had talked many times with Meg, advising her with such sympathy and understanding.

'Tell about the wicked fairy.' Lisa snuggled into the duvet for safety, so that only her bright, half-frightened eyes gazed at Meg.

'Seats of honour had been set for the seven fairy godmothers—'

'Auntie Zilla was my fairy godmother.'

'Godmother.' What an irony.

'Will Auntie Zilla be my – my spare mummy now?'

Meg quelled the questions by reading on: 'To the dismay of everyone, there appeared in the doorway an old crone, dressed in black and leaning on a crutched stick. Her chin and her hooked nose almost met together, like a pair of nutcrackers. She growled to the guests in a terrible voice 'I am the Fairy Uglyane!'

If only Zilla had been ugly, or fat, or even faithful. If only she could have seen into Zilla's mind. How was it that she'd never felt the slightest frisson of worry? She must have been as credulous as this child who believed in fairies. 'One of the younger fairies overheard her mumbling threats between her teeth and hid herself close by the cradle so that she might have the last word and undo what evil the Fairy Uglyane might have in her mind.'

'Evil, weevil, weevil evil,' intoned Lisa, beginning to get sleepy at last.

Meg read through the list of virtues bestowed upon the Princess Aurora and thought how the needs of women had changed since Quiller-Couch's day. Beauty and wit were still useful, but you needed much more than the abilities to dance, sing and 'play exquisitely on all instruments of music'. Today's woman was expected to be successful in her career, materially wealthy, perfectly packaged, sexy, and maternal as well. See the *Dallasty* soaps for the stereotype 'princess' of today.

'This is my gift to you, Princess Aurora,' announced the hag, in her creaking voice that shook as spitefully as her body. 'One day you shall pierce your hand with a spindle, and on that day you shall surely die!"' Meg wished she could pierce Zilla's white hands with spindles, scratch out her puppy-dog eyes, scrape bloody talons across her peach-down cheeks and yank out handfuls of her limp blonde hair.

She looked at her sleepy daughter and wondered how the happenings of today would affect her in the future. She didn't want to parent single-handed – the job was hard enough with two of you. 'The fair Hippolyta stepped forth from behind the tapestry saying 'Instead of dying, she shall fall into a deep slumber that shall last for many years, at the end of which a King's son shall come and wake her.'

What fantasy. Soon Lisa would sleep. Then she, Meg, would have to face alone the events of this day. Softening her voice, she read on. Anything to stave off the unbelievable facts. 'After the wicked witch had taken her departure, the palace fireworks were duly set off.'

Lisa mumbled 'I didn't like the bangs at Auntie Zilla's party. Daddy was brave.'

'Where will you go?' Meg had asked 'Daddy'. 'To Zilla's?'

'I have taken a room,' he had said, 'till the divorce is through. It will be less awkward for Zilla and the children.'

Less awkward for Zilla? Meg hadn't been able to believe this conversation was actually taking place, so her voice had sounded quite normal, as in discussing the neighbour's cat.

'Teenagers, you know. Zilla feels it would be difficult for them to explain to their friends.'

'Of course,' she had replied conversationally. You were trained to stay calm in times of stress, taught not to show your emotions in public – it was bad form. 'It wouldn't just be easier for you to stay on here till you –'

'No.'

So keen to escape, to break their tie. So anxious for Zilla's peace of mind, so careless of Meg's torn and bleeding heart.

'Mummy, you've stopped.' Lisa wriggled deeper under the duvet. Broken families caused delinquency, truancy, even drug-addiction these days. Meg herself had been known to explain away a difficult student, Oh he comes from a broken home...

She read on doggedly, paraphrasing, telling in her own words how the King came galloping home to the Palace. Would 'Daddy' gallop home in his white hatchback and help out in a crisis? What would happen if she got ill, couldn't cope with Lisa? Childish weakness washed over Meg for an instant, but she dammed it back, keeping it for later, forcing her mind to concentrate on the task in hand. 'Hippolyta arrived at the Palace in a fiery chariot drawn by dragons.' Veronica in her Porsche. Later tonight she could phone

Veronica, tell her 'Daddy' had finally gone. Then she might begin to believe the impossible truth of it herself. 'That very instant they all fell asleep.'

There was no escaping the fact that she was now reading to a sleeping child. To sleep, perchance to dream. Meg's thoughts began to drift more wildly: there were the sleeping tablets – would death be an easy way out, or would you be haunted for all eternity by the fact you had left your child motherless as well as fatherless? Yet suicide seemed, somehow, too dramatic a gesture. She lacked the conviction, and the courage. Lisa would need a mother, in double strength, to care for her. Anyway, to do away with your life for one rotten man could be to over-react.

Other people had survived divorce – maybe she would. It was just that at this moment she lacked the confidence. It wasn't as if 'Daddy' had beaten her, or anything dramatic like that. Guilt riddled her like woodworm. Agony columns said that people only strayed because Something Was Wrong At Home – in other words their partners, meaning wives, were useless in bed. But Meg's brain suggested, on the contrary, that possibly there was something wrong with him. Counsellors promised that if she would only ride out the storm, the fairy-tale ending could still be hers. How many women constituted a storm? When the known count had reached a dozen, Meg's patience had run out. With her self-esteem at zero, she'd indulged in a meaningless affair herself. It had boosted her ego a notch or two – and doubled her burden of guilt, for now she was colluding in the break-up of the family, was she not?

The confusing thing was that, illogically, she still loved 'Daddy'. She loved his sunny nature, devoid as he was of all introspection, even though it rendered him incapable of talking through problems – he simply denied their existence. How tenderly she loved every detail of him, the way his hair curled on his neck, his smell, his strong hands. Part of her wanted desperately to feel secure in his ability to take care of things as her father had done, but he wouldn't play that role, couldn't follow the rules of her game. In spite of everything, she could not blame him – he was a helpless male, caught in the web of another woman's wiles.

It was Zilla she hated, with green vitriolic loathing. For four years Zilla had been carrying on a double life that would have defied the detection methods of MI5 – not that Meg had been suspicious. It had been quite by chance that, one difficult day when she had been feeling particularly aggrieved she had remarked, 'Who's the current fancy then?' And he'd replied 'Zilla. I thought you knew.' 'Of course,' she had lied. And her mind had clamped shut while she heard her voice developing a life of its own, going on as if she were chatting to a stranger at a party. Apparently Zilla needed him, being the helpless type, not capable like Meg.

Only later, when her head defrosted in a scarlet heat of embarrassment, anguish and fury, had she begun to remember all the times she had confided in Zilla – all these confessions about 'Daddy's' infidelities, given freely over a stream of coffee cups and wine-glasses. Zilla had listened, and listened. Now Meg imagined Zilla as a huge red ear drinking in every vital clue about 'Daddy'.

'Mummy, you've stopped.' Lisa's eyes prised themselves open a chink. 'Finish my story?'

'Within a few hours there grew up around the palace such a tangle of briars and undergrowth that neither man nor beast could find a passage.' Meg's voice droned into automatic pilot again. Never again would she believe anything a man said to her. Men were beasts. You couldn't trust women either.

'Daddy' had gone. The actual going had been so clear, so final, and yet so utterly unbelievable. He had come home from the office, packed a case, taken the lamp from his side of the bed, his pillow, his book, his clock, a few photographs from the bedside drawer, and put them in his car.

'Do you mind if I take the ship painting?' he had asked in his everyday voice.

How could she mind? He had bought it.

'And a couple of plates and things?'

He had to eat. She noticed how pale and drawn he looked. 'Help yourself,' she said, evenly. 'Would you like – the meal's ready – before you go?'

'No.'

He had gone then, out the front door, the cord from his shaver trailing like some torn umbilicus, the old washbag he'd had at boarding-school clutched to his chest like a teddy.

'Won't you kiss me goodbye?' She had accompanied him as far as the door, not wanting to embarrass him, keeping her dignity, offering her cheek.

'I think not.' He had walked on.

She had seen the quick glance he gave the neighbouring windows as he shoved his gear awkwardly into the hatchback. Then he was starting the engine. For an instant the farcical nature of the situation had threatened to engulf Meg in hysterical giggles. She had pinched her mouth shut, had waved, drowning, as he drove away down the road and merged with the confusion of traffic.

For a long time she had stood completely numb, Lot's wife, a pillar of salt, too dry for tears, a huge lump of indigestible agony inside her.

The child's voice needled its way into her consciousness. As soon as Lisa's demanding child mind was switched off for the night Meg would be without defence. The realisation that she would probably be alone for a long time bled into her brain till she could no longer stem the flow of thought.

She began to examine how exactly she felt and, to her astonishment, discovered the merest trickle of relief. The uncertainty was behind her. Ahead lay the rest of her life, in which she was going to be free to do exactly what she liked. Through the pain of loss grew the realisation that this would include possibilities: some scary, some exciting, some plain silly. No longer would a man's heavy sighs pull at her guilt-complexes, make her run to fetch snacks to bribe him to stay at home. He had gone. It was too late. She had tried her best – and failed.

She could paint the whole flat pink if she felt like it, laze undisturbed in bed, spend holidays in Mull instead of Corfu, join the Green Party without ruining anyone's 'reputation.'

And tonight? Tonight she would phone Veronica, fix a date to tell her everything. She would relax with a book by the fire, not television with all its lies about washing up making your hands fairy-soft, its unbelievably perfect homes, its preference for processed coffee, its fantasy marriages. In her failure lay the seeds of real happiness, maybe even success. Unburdened, she would have peace of mind to concentrate on her work, at last. This child would be an anchor, helping to keep her steady. Gently stroking Lisa's hair, she read softly on about Prince Florimond hunting in the forest, magically finding a pathway through the tangled briars to the sleeping Palace. 'He climbed the grand staircase and found the most beautiful Princess lying fast asleep on a bed. He fell in love with her at first sight and sank to his knees to kiss her hand that lay, light as a rose leaf, on the coverlet.'

'Mummy?' Lisa rolled over.

'Shsh, it's nearly finished. 'They were married there and then and lived –'

'What's for breakfast?'

'Porridge.' The realities of every day. Meg tucked the duvet round the little pink cheek. Maybe everyone needed fantasies, needed a way of explaining away the incomprehensible sadnesses we each have to suffer. This dreadful day was nearly over. Idly she turned to the next story. Once upon a time –. Oh, what use were stereotypes of helpless princesses, dashing princes, dream marriages, when in reality you began your adult life with a flawed personality, which selected the wrong man, for the wrong reasons, who then let you down and left you high and dry with his child. Things didn't come right by magic. She shut the book. Tomorrow would begin soon enough.

## A WORD FOR LOVE

*AMO AMAS*, I loved a lass, and she was tall and slender – 'love' was a word used to joke with, until we reached the age for it. Now romantic love accounts for the work-load of hundreds of counsellors, shelvesful of psychology books, columns of words by palm-readers, astrologers, hand-writing experts, and an entire publishing industry – witness the Mills & Boon phenomenon. Meantime whole generations of mystified people have their shampoo, their instant coffee, their car and their alcohol sold to them because they connect these things with being loved.

What do *you* love? Everything from tomato ketchup to your new baby? From having your back scratched 'just there' to a brilliant bit of sex with your lov*er*? Your cat, your dog, your pet performing flea – or the money in your bank-balance?

How many kinds of love are there? Germaine Greer explains that we use the notion of romantic love to dress up egotism, masochism and lust. Love, she suggests, is a fantasy cloaked in mythology and girded about with sentimentality which leads us to behave in certain ways – the 'frozen gestures of courtship... the kissing and the dating... the compliments and the quarrels' of being in love, which result in a roller-coaster of self-induced joy and misery under which the essential personality disappears. Clearly she thinks love is not good for us.

And yet we like to love.

If only we had different words to express each sort of love, we might be less mixed-up about it – and less easily conned.

For instance, is that feeling of being legless with man-lust 'love'? Or merely a physical phenomenon – Mother Nature catching us out with her hormone cocktail again, doing her best to get us on the mat so that the human race continues to exist? Is it possible that this delirium we feel for an exciting new man – that lethal mix of churning physicality and the wondrous realisation that we must have been a pair of swans – or maybe even ducks – in some previous existence – truly love?

And if it is, then what exactly is it that you feel for your child? That strange mixture of protection, envy, frustration, irritation, selflessness and self-congratulation we feel about our offspring? Surely not – that's taboo, and dangerous territory – look what happened to Oedipus. If different, why have we never concocted a word to contain them? Don't these experiences merit words of their own?

How do other cultures cope? Do the Inuit, who have at least ten different words for different types of snow, have more to say about love? Seemingly not. And the French even confuse the words 'love' and 'like' so that they have to be girded about with adjectives for some degree of clarity to emerge. For surely they don't feel the same for their Camembert as they do for their Dior, their Marseillaise, their poodle? Even French self-esteem is 'amour propre'.

They can laugh at us, too, for inconsistency. In English 'love' means nothing, zero, no score, especially in tennis.

And 'making love'? Surely that is an impossibility? 'Making love' for Victorians meant making eyes, holding hands, rarely kissing. Now we use the term as a euphemism for sexual intercourse, although that's confusing, because sexual intercourse need have nothing whatever to do with emotion, being sometimes simply the satisfaction of a strongly-felt physical appetite – more like a good curry to a Weightwatcher than a spiritual experience.

Then again, people of different religious persuasions are expected to 'love' various deities – Allah, Jehovah or whoever – something so ethereal that you can neither sleep with it, nurture it nor eat it. Surely religious love merits a special word, one which accurately expresses the feelings of those who believe. Even Gerard Manley Hopkins had difficulty – and he was a poet who could do amazing things with words. In his desperate efforts to make the English language do what it was incapable of, to express God-love, what came out was gratitude: 'Glory be to God for dappled things', 'The tide that ramps against the shore.' There are times when his writing looks like the rantings of a child who cannot get a toy to work properly.

Of course there's more choice in Scots or Gaelic. Acair's Gaelic dictionary lists no less than twelve lilting words for love, any one of which would gladden a maiden's lug – roll your tongue around gràidhean, mo ghràdh, càirdeas. In Scots you can be wooed with words like amouris, drowry, fainness, floan, gyte, kirr, or simply get the smuirich or hert-likin before you swoon into his arms.

So 'love' remains a loose, unsatisfactorily catch-all term, like 'pudding.' If you're in Yorkshire, pudding is savoury and used to fill you up so you don't eat too much meat. If it's in Glasgow, puddings are black and bloody, fried full of cholesterol and served up in newspaper dripping with tomato ketchup. Anywhere in Britain it's syrup stodge, or sorbet, or semolina – or crepes Suzette. I think 'love' should be banned. It's a four-letter word. *Amo amas* – alas.

# *SHADOWS FALL*

THE SOUND OF THE KETTLE strains into the silence. A floorboard creaks under my pink-slippered foot. I go through the comforting routine of tea-brewing; real leaves, none of your old bags for me. Especially not on a morning like this, after a night like that.

In the dark hall behind me the grandmother clock brassily announces 5 am. And he's still up there. What ought I to do? Something, surely, if I'm a mother worth the name.

All night I have been lying awake thinking of Marie my daughter, trying to visualise what my mother would have done in similar circumstances. I failed. The situation simply could not have arisen.

Things were so different then, and in some ways worse. A curfew operated in our house when I was sixteen. In by nine, unless there were exceptional cirumstances like a school dance, and then it was extended only till eleven. My young men had seen me home, given me an inexpert peck in a doorway on the way, and left the minute my father opened the front door. For I had learned, painfully, that my father had to be obeyed. With apparent docility, I evolved a way of surviving his rules, so strong was the call of young life out there in the real world. I would listen for his snores, then I would shin down a well-placed drainpipe to join whatever party was going on. Johnny and I slept rough under the trees one night. Later I'd clamber back up the wall in the small hours, certain that my father would hear my very heartbeats. He never did. In the end poor Johnny had to marry me. It was the way in those days, when a girl fell pregnant.

Now, in these new small hours, is Marie making the same mistake? My ears reach into the dark house, trying to find sounds that will tell me something, hearing nothing.

I look again at the note. Marie had left it on the kitchen table for me – she often left notes for me if she came in first. Last night I had been late after a reunion with school-friends of yesteryear. It was beautifully written in her round neat hand, as usual.

'Hi Mum,' it said. 'I'm in. Hope you had a good time with the Ancients – 2 Alkaseltzer below attached. Mike's staying the night in my room. I'll be leaving early for swimming practice – try not to waken you. 'Night, sleep well. XXX.'

'Now now, young man, you must get up and leave this house immediately. Never darken our door again.' Should I have marched up to her room and delivered such a speech, wielding the garden spade to protect my daughter's honour?

Or, at sixteen, is she now an adult, free to make her own choices, her own mistakes?

She had been my mistake. Not my only one, but the one with the farthest-reaching consequences. It had been such a struggle to rear her after Johnny left home. We'd managed, with difficulty, she and I. Oh the hardness of the choice I'd had to make; to go to work leaving her alone in the house if she was ill, or to risk losing the job by staying at home, and going without the low part-time wage that fed and clothed us and paid the rent. She'd been such a difficult, resentful creature in her middle teens. Now she was just beginning to flower into an assured, hard-working, frank young woman.

So frank that I knew her views on religion – no such thing as God; politics – she was the last feather on the edge of the left wing; and sex – she wasn't going to mess about with her hormones by taking the Pill, and anyway the Pill was no protection against AIDS.

I, knotted with inhibition, gnarled with guilt on the subject of anything physical, had struggled to inform her on the barest facts of life. A book, tastefully coloured pink-for-girls, left lying around, had, I hoped, filled in the gaps caused by my inadequacy; I had been utterly incapable of managing words like masturbation or penis.

Drink the tea. Calm streaking nerves. Turn on the radio to blank out thought. That's it, gentle music. Six chimes on the grandmother clock. He's still up there, that spiky-headed boy. In Marie's – bed? How naive to imagine, in these permissive days, that he'd be anywhere else. I must steel myself for the worst.

Marie had introduced him to me last December before the school Christmas disco. Now he was in sixth year with her, just one of her large gang of friends I had thought. Normally they would all spend Friday or Saturday evenings together in one of other of their family homes, playing music, talking, drinking 7 Up or cider. When it was our turn, one or two of her girlfriends would stay the night; she'd do the same after an evening at theirs. But Marie had never mentioned this boy, Mike, particularly – or had I not been listening properly?

Sometimes, as she rattled through all the minutieae of her day, my mind would slide away to dwell on some problem of my own – a bill I couldn't pay, a lecture I had to write. Marie had her own life to live. With a bit of luck she'd make a better job of hers than I had of mine. Things were easier now, for a girl. She'd do well in her exams, perhaps get into University to study Pharmacy – her Saturday job at the chemist's would help her eke out her grant. Unlike me, she had the chance of a good career ahead of her. She would have no need to hunt for some unreliable man to keep her, no need to hurry into marriage. No need to marry at all? And children?

She was frank about children, too. Couldn't abide them. Said she for one wasn't going to add to the overpopulation of the world and have her life eaten up by any puking, leaky brat. But I remember how tenderly she loved her hard and unresponsive doll. She has a deep well of warmth to give, to someone, some day, for all her outward cynicism.

Now I must steel myself to go, must go treading up thes stairs, must go into her bedroom and stop, yes, stop this spiky youth from doing any more, any further harm to my own, my darling daughter.

Fury lights my way. Pink suede slippers hush my tread on the stair carpet. Outside Marie's I door stop for an instant, listening, and I feel like a criminal, a spy, an intruder. I reach for the door-handle.

Alarm bells scream, rattling my nerve. I back away, turn and run, weeping hot tears. Downstairs again in the kitchen I shut the door behind me and lean against it, heart thumping, trying to catch my breath, regain control.

Someone is coming, is treading downstairs. How will I face him, them? There is a long yawn. The door is pushed against me. I move away.

She's wearing the worn-out pink kaftan she 'borrowed' a lifetime ago last night. 'Any tea left in the pot, Mum? What're you doing up so early?'

'Your note,' I mumble, my hand shaking the tea-pot so a little spills on the table. 'Michael?'

'Oh he's out for the count. Hope you didn't mind – I bunged him in the sleeping-bag. He's so thick he'll not feel the floor. I'll dig him out when I get back from the baths, OK? Yuk this tea's cold. Shall I make you some fresh? You look awful – must've been quite a party! The Ancients all still surviving? Oh, Jenny and I are going to watch the rugby at ten – Mike's playing for the first, and Andy and Jim. We're at Jenny's tonight, remember . . .?'

The kettle whistles. Outside the sun is beginning to rise. A blackbird sings on the clothes pole.

# *LONG WINTER SUNDAY*

'HEY MA! Come on, we're nearly at the top. Look!'

Muffled, numb, I plod uphill in deep snow. Wrapped in thick knitting, scarfed, gloved, socked and booted I feel nothing. The ski-goggles insulate my eyes, the hood my ears. Proof against all feeling, I trudge upwards. There is a long way still to go.

Pigeon breasts of snow feathered with fawn grasses quilt the hillside. The father's black figure kicks bootsteps into the hill-flank above me. The brothers scramble up, and slide down a little with each footfall. Two of my sons.

'Ma, look, this rock's completely covered in ice. Ouch! I'll exterminate you, creep!'

'Try it, big hero. I'm going to be at the top first, ha!'

Two sons. Always fighting, vying with each other for success, for attention, yet good friends, separated by only a year.

Their voices sound bare, without resonance in the frozen air. There is no wind on this side of the mountain. Is Dumgoyne a mountain? Or merely a molehill? There is the cairn, looking like a birthday cake, whiffs of snow streaking off the top like ribbons. We'll feel the wind up there all right, high against the wide blue sky.

But I have three sons. The third should be snug in the carrying sack on my shoulders. I lack his weight on my back. On previous Sunday walks his small body has kept me warm, and I him. The sack hangs empty on the kitchen hook.

The father and the two brothers are together above me. He is pointing out distant landmarks, which they can see but I cannot, still pressed against the hillside. They seem oblivious, so close in their maleness, forgetful so soon.

Voices. My mother: 'The family – you're so lucky. A nice home, enough money, a good man who works hard to keep you all. You should be grateful.' A friend: 'The boys – you must pull yourself together, for their sakes.' My father: 'Your husband. Look to him. He bears the burden of responsibility for you all just now. You can't let him down.'

The hill steepens. One foot slips, then the other. I slide downwards grabbing with smothered, clawless fingers. All my efforts are wasted and I land in a heap at the bottom of the slope. It is impossible, I lack the equipment, and the determination, to try again. Slow tears leak through the goggles and freeze on my cheeks. I have not cried at all, till now.

I look up. The three of them are busy, making snowballs. They laugh as they begin to fling soft flurries down at me, squealing if they make a direct hit. Suddenly I hate them, the smiling father, the frolicking, forgetful boys.

The father has smiled on other women. For the sake of the children I have chosen not to notice these leerings – and for myself. But the family has been ripped apart now. These boys have no need of me – they live in a man's world of hard metal cars and fighting. The cars are matchbox size but will grow bigger, the fights are part of school playground life, of street life too. In a few brief years they'll slough me off – the old woman – in favour of freedom, the struggle to make their own marks on the world. Then younger women will take them from me. What is the point of organising my life around them? What is the point of climbing this stupid hill? Because it is there?

And the little one, the dependant, my baby. This time seven Sundays ago I was holding his warm hand, by the hospital bed. Later, at noon, they took away the useless plastic tent and all the life-saving gear. At twelve minutes past, he died. His live hand died in mine. I, who had first felt the flutter of his tiny life within me, alone, in private, had been condemned to feel his last small breath alone too. I alone bore my little child company in his passing, for him, for myself and to protect the family from anguish, for his father who couldn't bear the grief. Born when the green buds opened, he lived only a leaf's length of time and in November died.

My mind tolls each dull fact one by one as it has done daily these past weeks, but today each intolerable blow strikes the very quick of my bare nerves till I press my goggled face into the snow and scream my agony, at last, into the bosom of the hillside.

Every day for three months I had driven to the hospital to care for him. Each darkening autumn day I had sung the twenty-third psalm over and over, as a prayer, a hope, a talisman – 'And tho' I walk through death's dark vale, yet wi-il I fear none ill, for thou art with me, a-and thy rod, and sta-aff me comfort still' – if I reached the end of that verse before passing a certain ploughed field, everything would be all right. Neither the prayer nor the talisman worked.

Now it is the very dead of winter. Men on the moon, they had said, yet this disease hasn't been researched. No cure – we'll try cortisone, it has worked on some American children, do you accept the risk? Then sign here. And my little son was killed by my acceptance of his risk.

White ribbons and premature snowdrops from a shop, a tiny white coffin like a cake, carried awkwardly by the black-coated stranger. Did I want him to be cremated or buried? I could have whatever I wanted, they said, as though I was arranging a christening, not a funeral. I wanted *him*. For three nights I stayed awake, alone with the choice between flames consuming, or worms devouring, the little hands, the perfect toes, the chunky baby body, the blue eyes of my darling. I picked Fire, in the end, for its cleansing speed. But buried, not scattered, is the small box of grey ash, so that one day my dead body may curl again round his, protecting him from the cold blast of eternity.

'One of God's flowers,' 'needed in Heaven', 'too good for this world,' the unctuous platitudes spilled from the mouths of church-wives, boosting their shaken beliefs. But he was needed here, here in my arms against my breast, sucking, warm, safe. And I had failed him in his mortal struggle, not strong enough to save him. No longer do I believe there is a benevolent watching eye, with plans and intentions for humanity. For me, God is now dead, an anachronism invented by people as a panacea for agonies they could not comprehend. And I am condemned to Life, because it is there.

'Are you coming up or not?' The father shouts from his ridge.

I look up. Another snowball hits me, square in the face. 'Bull's eye, Dad! You got her.'

Anger flares, taking me by surprise. I strip off the steamed-up goggles, pull back the deafening hood, rip off the insulating gloves. I will climb this hill, to the brim.

More snowballs fall around me. I move around the base of this, the last slope, find a place where icicle-laden bushes thrust through, and where no foot has trodden. Here my boots grip more surely the frosted crust, the whiteness squeaking under my weight as I climb, slowly at first, gripping bramble stems, thorns and all, with my bare hands to haul myself up. So steep is the final pitch that the sharp snow-smell prickles my nostrils from right in front of my face. I scuffle two handfuls into a ball and hurl it blindly up towards the summit.

'Hey, look, Ma's going to make it. Stop the bombing!'

'O.K, O.K. C'mon old Ma, we'll give you a pull.'

My blood heats with effort, my breath gusts dragonlike puffs of steam. I lean for a moment on iced rock. The top pitch looks perpendicular, impossible, the North Face of the Eiger. I dare not look back now, or down. Too far to fall. Other women have been here before me, I say to myself. Other women have reached the summit, suffered and overcome. Three children out of Grandmother's dozen sickened and died in childhood. I used to think that in those olden days the women must have expected to lose a proportion of their children, must have become inured to loss. I do not think so now. How often had dark skeletal women stared at me from dusty television screens over the stick-limbed bodies of their dying children? I had believed it must be almost their normal state, their babies dying daily. I do not think so now.

Pushing off again, upwards towards the skyline, I wonder what I have done to deserve my two remaining, rudely healthy sons?

Now the snow has been flayed away by the wind. Tussocks of stiffened grass stick to juts of stone, and hidden under a ledge, green velvet moss cushions my bleeding fingers. As I grip the top edge, sunshine warms my shoulders.

'You two push, I'll pull.' The father's black-gloved hand reaches down to me and four smaller hands shovel me over the last rock. For a minute I lie on my belly, gasping with expended effort. 'Well done,' he says.

'Look, Ma, I'm going even to the top of the cairn!'

Meanwhile his brother has scrambled up and stands there among the stones, triumphant against the blue sky. A fight ensues. My grateful ears hear the wind-song of two swans, flying low, winging between this hill and the next, pristine, unscathed.

Standing up, I catch the freezing wind. I do not care, for

I can see clearly all the wavy edges of my circular horizon, being at its middle. 'I will lift mine eyes unto the hills from whence cometh my aid.' Eastward lie the Campsies. Straight ahead runs the dark valley of the Blane. Murky fog blankets Glasgow, stuck with concrete peg-blocks, laced with pylon wires. Westward, low hills dip to reveal a sliver of Loch Lomond, and beyond a cylcorama of crisp peaks reaches to the muscular shoulder of the Ben.

Below the snow-line all the hills are furred with woods, kilted with pines, wrapped in the warm bronze of bracken, patched and padded with green fields. So small and insignificant am I, invisible to anyone standing on any of these landscapes, yet for a few brief years, however inadequate, privileged to be at the centre of my children's existence.

'Look, boys, that's where we live.' I begin to point out landmarks they can recognise, their father naming distant mountains: 'The Cobbler, see? Ben An.' They are cold now, so we encircle them for warmth and share a chocolate bar.

We slither downhill towards the westering sun till the snow-line wanes. We plouter thigh-high through tangled heather clumps down to the bracken. The birch wood smells of damp mosses and decay as we follow an old track down to the waiting car. Inside, it steams up as we drive home.

'Can we have a fire?' The boys carry logs in from the shed and their father, my husband, makes scarlet and gold flames crackle cheerfully, chasing away the chill. Woodsmoke follows me from the imperfect chimney into the kitchen.

Standing by the warm grill I de-frost, making toast, spreading it piece by piece with melting butter, brown sugar, drifts of bracken-coloured cinnamon. Outside, beyond the window, the sun slides blue shadows across the garden, and I see the first snowdrop, green and white, gleaming above the black earth.

# *MY SON, MY SON*

'WELL. THAT'S HIM AWA' Her brown eyes burn briefly into mine over the edge of her cup.

I know what she means, but say 'Have another biscuit before you start? So, he's off to Ireland?' A branch of the thorn tree taps on the window like a bony finger. Wind streaks rain across the garden. I turn on Radio One. I am being deliberately dim, to put off the unthinkable thing she's going to tell me, because I can't bear to hear it.

'Tae the Gulf.'

'But I thought his lot were due for a tour in Ireland?' A tour. It sounds like something from Holiday '91. Insipid pop music fills the silence.

Jackie takes out another cigarette. Her hand shakes the lighter so that she has to concentrate to steady the flame. She drags smoke into her lungs, as if it were courage? 'They never got tae Ireland. They got sent straight tae Saudi.'

'When?' There's no escape. I have to hear her through this. We have so much in common, Jackie and I. We both hate ironing, we both love bright colours, and we are both the mothers of sons. For the time being, my son sleeps.

'Ah got word on Friday. They just phoned and telt me. Like that. Some weekend Ah hud.'

'Did you speak to Iain?'

'Ye must be jokin'. Naw. It wis this wumman. I says tae her 'Weel hen, I wouldnae hae your job.' That's whit she hus tae dae. She hus tae phone a' the faimlies and tell them their sons is aff tae war. Then, if – somethin' happens, you know – she hus tae phone them. Us. And tell us, like. She says 'I'm your contact with Iain, for everything.'

Jackie can think of another woman's feelings at time like this?

'Louie's her name. She says tae call her Louie, it's no' sae formal and that, she says. She says 'Iain wouldn't put his things away. All the others packed and labelled their effects, but Iain said 'I'll be back, you'll see.'

'She says 'Iain is very mature. He understands where he's going and what it's all about.' My God. She should have saw Iain afore he joined up. Mature? Eighteen and no' workin'. Comin' hame a' oors o' the nicht, and God knows whit he's been up tae. Ah couldnae control him. Yon day the polis came roon. 'Time you wis oot, son' Ah says. 'Time you were oot roughin' it a bit, at your age. Ye'r a man noo. No a wean. On yer way,' Ah says. 'And don't come back till ye've made somethin' o' yersel.'

'You put him out of the house?'

'Aye Ah did. A grown man. Time he wis staunin' on his ain feet, no trampling a' ower mine.' Her voice cracks in the effort to sound harsh.

'So, he got into the army.' This is safe, known territory we've been over before. Jackie loves to talk about Iain. He is her only child. And my son is upstairs. Oh he's not lazy. He's a good student. The cistern flushes. He will be with us any minute, tousled and slow with sleep. He is the light of my life. His growing up, his warmth and laughter have given me such years of joy. I obliterate the sounds of his approach with talk. 'Remember last year – Iain's Passing Out?'

'Ah wis that feart, travellin' there on ma ain.'

'Have you the photo, still?' I know she's never without it. Jackie fishes in her bag. She produces a small glass frame, the picture I've seen before. Iain stands tall and stiff beside her, she dressed in her best, looking self-conscious, he expressionless under the army hat, anonymous, like any other soldier. 'It's him.' She smiles with such tenderness and vulnerability. 'Like – it's his eyes. Ye know?'

I try to keep Jackie on this comfortable track – for her peace of mind, or mine? To help her forget where he is now. Would anything make me forget if – ? As she talks, TV newsreels flicker through my mind, helicopter gun-ships, dealing death over Khafji. I'd always thought of helicopters as quaint, kindly, helpful. Helicopters rescued fallen climbers, shipwrecked fishermen, men off burning oil-rigs. Now they spat death from the sky like malevolent insects. Another picture, of a young Iraqui conscript giving himself up. He's crouched against the base of a wooden post, three young Brits surrounding him, their guns pointed at his heart. His brown spaniel eyes look up at them, expecting death. Does his mother see him on her screen?

Why is he there? Why are any young people there? War is the result of bungling by our generation and our parents', not by these young people. Centuries ago Lysistrata and her women persuaded their husbands to stop fighting, by using sexual blackmail, yet still we try to solve world problems with human blood. Is the idea of peace merely a luxury, like health foods and animal welfare, used to fuel endless discussions by idealistic students, the loony left, and the middle classes?

I keep talking. 'You were so proud of Iain that day, weren't you?' What makes women feel pride when their sons are sent into battle. What on earth is there to be proud of?

Jackie always looks straight at you. Her eyes are goldy-brown with very bright whites, and they normally express a kind of ironic humour.

'Aye, Ah wis.' She's almost excusing herself for loving Iain. 'His eyes. Disnae maetter whit he's done. He just luiks at ye. He's that wey – ye cannae help but love him.' She shrugs and drags in more smoke, doomed. 'I've even wrote him a letter. It's nae good greetin'. His pal's Mammy – she's writing a' this sob-stuff, aboot missin' him and that. Whit good's that gonny dae the boy? He's no wantin' tae hear a' her worries, is he?'

'So, what do you write about?'

'Ah telt Iain aboot Nancy up the sterr.'

'Nancy who's pregnant?'

'Aye. Well, Ah telt him, she's got that big on top, ye know, she canny get a bra tae fit her. I says 'see us a perr o' yer helicopters son, wan tae haud up each side o' Nancy, otherwise she's gonny trip ower hersel on the sterr yin o' these days.' Ah just tell him onythin that comes intae ma heid. It disnae metter if it's true or no', sure it doesnae?' He's no wantin' tae hear aboot ma worries, is he?'

She searches the tea-leaves in her empty cup. 'They'd tae make their wills. Yon Louie telt me. Ye know, in case . . .'

I think of Iain, at last. What does he believe he is fighting for? He has no religion, and this is no Crusade for some misplaced principle. He probably has more personal grudge against a boy from the next scheme than against any Iraqi. The jaunty voice of a Radio One newsreader speaks of the invasion of Iraq. How eagerly he promises chemical attacks, as though reporting the next instalment in some space adventure. These commentators scoop their livings like vultures from the terrible piles of burned and twisted bodies, from the debris of human misery and degradation, drooling over the anguished screams of the bereaved. I switch to Radio Scotland and McGregor's Gathering. Hamish Imlach is singing the old pacifist song 'I didnae raise ma son tae be a soldier'.

When he was little, I tried to talk peace to my son. Hopefully, I discouraged him from fighting his friends with any sort of implement and gave him no toy guns. Have I made him a freak? Soft? Have I made him anything? He is an individual, not my plaything. My father fought in a war, yet I am a pacifist. My son may well react against my ideals as he grows. And Jackie. Was it Jackie who forced her son to become a soldier?

Should I now feel shame in the face of her pride? If not, then why do I feel a blush rising over my face as my son shuffles into the kitchen, his chest bare over his torn jeans, all his movements so gentle and easy. He kisses me on the cheek, squeezes my shoulder and smiles at Jackie. He doesn't speak while he brews coffee and cooks himself a bowl of porridge. I am conscious of his presence, embarrassed as though I'd been caught showing off stolen goods.

Who made the decision about which boy stays at home and which goes to war? And might I ever find it my turn to be in her position? What if there's a call-up? Conscription? I say anything, anything to keep the terrible thought at bay. 'What made Iain choose the army?'

A long plume of grey smoke fogs the table. Her voice is tight. 'Choice? Whit choice dae ony o' us huv where Ah come fae? If they'd only gave us decent hooses. If the weans had hud a place tae play. If there'd been jobs for them when they left the schule. It wis that or nothin'. He gets a trainin', some discipline, his claes and his food. Ah thought – like Ah said – Ah couldnae sort him oot masel', ye've saw the height o' him – can ye see me tellin' him aff? But I thought maybe the army could – could dae somethin' fur him, make somethin' o' him maybe.'

My son looks from one face to the other, and frowns as he throws a jersey over his head and takes his jacket off the peg. 'Wake up, Ma,' he says. 'You're far away. I'm off to give blood, before the march. It's for the soldiers. Don't forget to put the Peace poster in the window, for Solidarity. Cheers, Jackie.' And he swings away out of the back door.

Jackie's brown eyes follow him like a dog's. They are dull, without expression, her thoughts battened down again, unreadable. She gets up from the table. 'Ah'd better get movin', hen.'

A cold wind blows through my kitchen.

# *WORKING MOTHERS, SCHOOL TERMS*

HOW BUSILY we conscien-
tious mothers of school-age
children constrict our lives to
accommodate school terms
and timetabling. We strain to fit our ambitions, juggle our
budgets, to an archaic, illogical system. Why?

We listen to complaints that so few women are involved
in politics, business, sport and the arts, that only a tiny
minority reach the top. Yet, until we actually have the *time*
to gain power in governmental bodies, how can we effect any
useful changes?

The trouble is that we're a modest lot. We have folkloric
notions of good motherhood, a partiality for the dominant
male – great chieftain o' the puddin' race – and every time we
trot meekly along to collect our children at the school gate
we endorse his monolithic organisation of State Education.

That can be one delivery and two collections twice daily.
Better than the Post Office.

Picture the good-wife of olden times, singing as she spins
her wool, minds her poultry, gathers her herbs, turns out a
batch of baking, and all with dozen children dangling from

her skirts. Cut to the year 2000 and visualise the House of Commons, with 50% of its membership composed of dynamic, highly educated, imaginative females, proportionately representing more of the same. Who are these women? From where have they come? And how are they to find time and energy to do the work?

This year of 1990 they may be our daughters, aged nine to nineteen. Are the most idealistic among them to be neutered, forbidden to complicate *their* lives with children, in order that we shall be represented?

Only the younger and more thoughtless feminist can truly believe that bunging children into a creche is sufficient to free the spirit. Few mothers doubt that their offspring have some kind of human right to parenting and a reasonable childhood. Someone might carry out a revealing survey into how many mothers opt merely for the *convenience* of school-work, simply to be available during the 'holidays', because of this. For *no* mother *likes* leaving her children unattended, roaming the streets.

'Human Scale Education' promoted by Small School enthusiasts is, like the Playgroup movement, parent-intensive. In most cases, for 'parent' read 'mother', who will thus have even less time to pursue her own career. Yet research shows that, far from having been liberated, we still come home from work to do most of the drudgery. Now, because insufficient funds are made available to schools, we're being persuaded to volunteer as educationalists.

Instead, shouldn't we mothers of tomorrow's women be insisting on something of more practical use?

Imagine a year during which there were no separate terms, in which huge urban schools opened all day as wonderful local resource centres in which you're free to use the vastly improved facilities for your children as much *or as little* as you want.

While there, your children aged 3-14 work in 'mini-school', human-scale groups fully staffed by professionals. A

medical team works in the well-equipped sick bay. A cafeteria
dispenses food all day. The needs of *children* come first, and
they lead full lives as well as learning. They progress through
school neither by age nor by a series of heavily documented
tests, but according to the demands and natural curiosities of
the child. In rural areas each community has a small unit
served by a large body of itinerant staff. Everything is 'free',
an investment from taxes in the future of Britain, diverted
perhaps from the now redundant Trident programme into
something rather more useful.

With time available in a quiet environment, children do
'homework' and those from overcrowded homes have a
better chance to study.

Courses are flexibly arranged in modules and options.
You take your children out of school when it suits *you*, and
them. The school hostel is available for brief stays, if your
work calls you away, or there's a crisis. Each establishment is
operated as a whole, because we have learned that it doesn't
work to have different bodies sharing the accommodation.

Who are the staff of these fabulous institutions? Teachers,
playleaders, counsellors, craftspeople and others.
Competitive salary scales and attractive conditions encourage
the most highly motivated people to apply. Opportunities
exist for part-timers, job-sharers and travelling experts.

Education in the new Secondaries is free for adults from
early teens to old age, *but compulsory for none*. We have at last
accepted that puberty is not always the optimum time to sit
life-deciding exams. Disaffected teenagers may now take
menial jobs, but these are a beginning, not a dead end. In
working with adults, rather than being herded in age-groups
with their peers, young people mature quickly, decide on
their own courses of action, having been given *more*
responsibility for their lives. They are regarded as *useful*
young *adults*. They may vote locally, and at sixteen in general
elections.

Truly comprehensive *facilities* for children would help

enormously in two ways: children, including future female high-achievers, would receive a fuller, more individually appropriate education, and working mothers would be freer to pursue their careers knowing their young were enjoying a satisfactory way of life, regardless of their circumstances. Whatever happens, we must push for fundamental changes to enable the most capable to reach the top, for it is imperative that women, including mothers, are freed to become decision-makers if we are to have sensible decisions made for other women.

We are to be, for a brief period, statistically necessary as workers. Education is paid for out of our earnings. We are *buying* the right to have it run in a useful way. As tax-payers, *we* invest in school buildings and know it's sensible to make full use of these.

Our children, including our daughters, are the worst educated in Europe. How can we alter this without radical and imaginative change?

# *MOVING ON*

6.0 A.M. Today I am going to be unfaithful. It will be my first time. I am driving down through the glen. This is the last full day of the summer term – my last day of freedom till Autumn. Although it is high summer, the sun hasn't yet fingered the dark furls of bushes in the hill crevices, and cobwebs still glisten in the hedgerows. Rabbits scatter across the road and dive for cover, terrified by my engine.

Everything is arranged. The children are to go up to the farm after school, and play with their friends there till I get home – part of a mutual child-minding service the farmer's wife and I operate. Tomorrow is prize-giving. And by tomorrow I will be a different woman, a wife who has cheated on her husband.

The loch is blank and opaque. It lies passively as I drift past on the road, not demanding my attention as I clatter along in my clapped-out, second, wife's car towards the town. How subtly we are devalued. He earns the money so he runs the Alfa-Romeo convertible. I who have borne the pain of producing the next generation, work at their rearing, am grateful for this rusting sardine-tinful of sputtering plugs and slashed seats. It's better than a bike – you can go further afield. You can go astray.

The Alfa and he live in town all week. They appear at weekends – unless there's competition from conferences or business-trips.

In the old days we all used to move back to the town for the winter – Autumn leaves in the park, ducking for Halloween apples, Christmas with the grandparents and skiing somewhere over the New Year holiday. In March I'd take the babies back to Argyll to watch the countryside blossoming, the coming of the lambs. The Alfa would come with friends to socialise over weekends. They'd go fishing or shooting in season and I'd cook huge meals, bake great loaves for the return of the hunters.

It was a good enough life. The difference between us was merely that he continued to improve his position at work – one of the youngest partners the firm had ever taken on, so brilliant, so committed, while I, quite happily out of the competitive stream, lost touch with the tensions of ambition, taking on instead the rhythms of the countryside, determining my day by the state of the weather, sowing and reaping according to season, rowing around in our bay, swayed by how the children felt like spending their day. Yet I was only ever half a country woman. I couldn't break a rabbit's neck, or hook a worm.

There had been no real sacrifice on my part. My ambitions were all physical, to mother vast numbers of children, to feed and rear them, to grow and plant and revel in the richness of the garden, to work at night with tactile silks and wools. This Alfa-owner could afford a full-time wife. Free to concentrate on his work, with sex and home-baking most weekends and his offspring cared for, he could work in peace, and for my lot I was, more or less, grateful.

When the youngest started school, Alfa presented me with this rusting car. It didn't strike me, at the time, that it could have been a guilt-present, the modern equivalent of the eternity-ring or the pearl necklace – it was too practical a gift for that. To cheer my lonely heart, I decided to spend one empty school day driving to town for some bookshop-browsing and coffee with my best friend. I'd surprise Alfa for lunch. I dropped into the town flat for the loo and a prink. The bed was rumpled. He must have been late for work, I thought, lifting the duvet to smooth the sheet.

At first I thought it was a cuff-link winking at me. Then I saw the hook. This huge earring, gold plastic in the shape of a serpent with a glass eye lay in his, my, our bed. My ears aren't pierced. I dislike jewellery. And I'm afraid of snakes.

This earring I had seen before, dangling from the neat lobe of my best friend's ear, the ear into which I was about to pour all my mundane anxieties, over coffee.

Alfa had always fooled around at parties and such, but I'd never seriously bothered. If he wanted to make an idiot of himself, let him – it was only because he'd drunk too much, again; it wasn't the real him.

For two long years I played out the charade of happy family life, for the sake of the children and, I suppose, because I was reluctant to disturb the enjoyable material elements of my life. I swallowed down the bile of anger, submitted to the humiliations that were heaped upon me, believing she would eventually bore him. Those two years dealt mortal blows to my self-esteem. So I decided to take myself back, to conduct my own affairs, take over the reins of my own life again.

9.0 a.m. The road has become a dual-carriageway. Wild roses still grow along the edges, with tamer ones from the Parks Department between, separating the flow of traffic. A railway line half-obliterates the view of the great river, which has wound its way from the heart of Scotland, rinsing her industrial sores and collecting all manner of filth from her civilised centre to pour past the half-dead shipyards here and pass outward to pollute the wild sea.

The first thing I needed to do was to find out if I was still physically attractive. The last thing I wanted was the complication of an emotional entanglement – love and romance had let me down and I no longer trusted their ideology. But women, surely, can only enjoy sex if they're in love – true, or false? I didn't want, either, merely to be the convenient depository for the fantasies of some inflated male ego. So I would conduct an experiment in human relations, with myself as the guinea-pig.

9.20 a.m. The Motorway. Normally one can do this section in minutes, but today there is a long contra-flow, so I am crawling along behind a Mother's Pride van.

Deliberately, I went window-shopping for the right man. He would have to be someone who appealed to me physically without being emotionally demanding. It became a hobby, keeping an eye open for an attractive healthy male I could like and respect, and who was unattached – for I would not cause another woman the anguish I had been through, for my own gratification. Last week I met him.

10.0 a.m. The thirty-mile-an-hour limit has been passed and I am in a stream of traffic behind a double-decker bus. You'd think the rush-hour would be over by now. The car is overheating again. A red traffic light stops me and I turn off the engine to let it cool.

I could turn back now. I haven't done anything – wrong – yet. At any moment until the moment of penetration I am still officially a faithful wife. The lights go to amber, and to green. I start up and move onward, towards the residential edge of the town centre. The appointment – one cannot exactly call it a date – is it an assignation? is for ten-thirty.

I have dressed quite carefully, feeling that jeans were not appropriate. Rather as I do when going to the doctor, needing to have arms, legs, and below-the-belt easy of access, I chose a flowery cotton dress, flimsy, feminine, but not sexy.

10.30 a.m. Parking in a Residents' Permit Only slot because all the legitimate places have been taken, I turn off the engine. It splutters, not wanting to stop, so I put it in gear and it lurches once then dies.

Take it slowly. No need to rush. You can still change your

mind. But my head has already done the forward-planning and it directs my feet towards the security door and my voice to utter the pass-word – my name – and my self up the three flights of stairs.

'I wasn't sure if you'd come,' he says, welcoming me with a light kiss, the sort of embrace friends give each other, not lovers.

We had only met the once, talked long into the night, found a certain rapport, he a keen conservationist, a lover of old poetry, with a lightness of touch that didn't bog you down in deep theory. He seemed interested in my views, my opinions too. And all evening a magnetism grew between us, an electricity that burned every time we made eye-contact, in each accidental brush of knee, hand, finger, that was purely physical.

11.0 a.m. We have had the coffee and some easy chat. He leads the way to the bedroom. I hesitate a moment, then follow. He does not know this is my first time, and I have tried to give him the impression that I am quite accustomed to the situation, not wanting him to feel responsible for my Fall from Grace. Does he suspect – does he care? Probably not. To get on with the job, I strip off my dress as I walk through the bedroom door, and while he's not looking. As he turns, I slip off my bra and briefs, then make a dive for the duvet, hiding myself playfully beneath it, peeping out at him daring him to follow me.

Thankfully he joins in the game, pulling his clothes off, and then we are fooling about like two kids, tossing pillows around, and finally kicking the duvet to the floor.

I have chosen well. He is most beautifully made, smooth brown skin over firm muscle, taut stomach, tiny buttocks, cocksure and oh so knowing of just where to touch, and how, and in what slow strokes, so cool at first, so light-fingered then so warming, so knowing of how long it takes to bring me to the brink of bliss, before he enters and I cry out, free to release my tension in a glory of sensation, no-one to hear, no-one to care about the noise I make.

4.0 p.m. Tea steams – he is bringing it to me as I come out of the shower and prepare to dress. 'Toast?' he says, buttering two thick slices, licking his fingers. I feel utterly relaxed, at peace. 'Next week?' he asks.

4.30 p.m. There's a parking-ticket on the windscreen. It has been worth every penny. The car chokes into life, gears whining as I pull away uphill.

The rush-hour is beginning, but I am lucky, all the lights are at green, and I drive gently, singing at the top of my voice some tune from the seventies – Eleanor Rigby – the Beatles.

4.50 p.m. The thirty m.p.h. limit flashes by – I am speeding, breaking the law! I am a Fallen Woman! Will I now slide down the slippery slope into other forms of criminality?

5.0 p.m. The Motorway contra-flow has been cleared. Revving up I charge along the fast lane. Maybe the Gods will cause me to crash, for I have sinned. I have sold my soul to the Devil as surely as Faust, in exchange for the knowledge I sought. I am an attractive woman. I have been told, on good authority, that I am terrific in bed. I have enjoyed the body of a man ten years younger than me, who is not hampered by a paunch, and whose breath does not reek of bad teeth and alcohol.

5.05 p.m. A roundabout ends the Motorway. I drive round it three times, for the Hell of it. I could go anywhere from here, north, south, east or west. I could go to the bad – but I feel so much better already.

I turn away from the town and head north up the dual carriageway.

5.15 p.m. I am still driving too fast. I swing on to the narrower road and head up towards the loch. The sun is bouncing off ripples caused by dozens of little boats, white hanky sails dot the blue, and a few picnickers are drifting towards their cars from the shore.

The children will be having their tea at the farm. I am looking forward to seeing them again. I have been away for a lifetime, it seems.

7.30 p.m. The sun is dropping below the mountains to the west and the tree-shadows stretch across the road. I have passed two caravans and a tour bus in the last ten minutes and now the road is my own. All the B & B signs have been covered over – full bedrooms everywhere at this time of year.

I am a different woman from the person who drove down this same road this morning. Nothing can ever be the same again. In an hour I shall be home. It won't be dark for a long time – sometimes daylight lingers till midnight at this time of year, and even beyond. The children and I will walk down from the farm along the old track, listening for the scuffle of night-creatures. Maybe we'll see the old badger, disturb the drinking deer at the well, tell ghost stories of long ago. I'll hear about their day, and who said what to whom, and who will get a prize tomorrow.

# THE HOUSE PLANT

YOU'VE GROWN TOO BIG for our space. Your leathery green tongues fill our room, air-roots spidering up our walls, a Monstera of a plant with legs. I chop your top off like an old cabbage, and put your roots to rot on our compost heap. But your stump remains in my hand, bleeding brown juice like vegetable blood.

Are you a cutting? Should I pot you up, to go on living in my living room, should I talk to you – or shut you up for good? Your stem-remnant sprouts one new leaf, lettuce-green, unfurling ready for Spring, one aerial root snaking, desperately seeking moisture in the desert of our carpet.

You're very old. You've spanned the reigns of two wives in this house. She bought you – she who grew her family in these rooms, and kept them neat and happy – she whose crab crawled, devouring her most fertile parts till she was all consumed.

I, the new wife, fed you, kept you going, alive for him and for her children – but you threatened to grow into all the corners of our life and for a while I longed to kill your evergreen memory and your invading shade.

Now your stalk ends curl – in pain? Your wound glistens white flesh globuled with jungle sap like treacle, winding down my arm.

He gives me breathing space and love, and keeps me warm – her family accept me now with grace and favours and their children only know her photograph you were trying to hide, on the wall. Now my shambles fills her space, my children squabble and munch in the kitchen, I keep him warm. Is she glad for him? The fears and insecurities are past.

I stick your cut in fresh compost, twine your last remaining root around the mossy stake, pour cooling water, spray your drooping leaf – and set you in the sun.

# MAIDEN VOYAGE

NICKY WANDERED AIMLESSLY down the beach and sat down beyond the shadow of the little stone quay. She drew a cross face in the sand. Charles was late, again.

Nearby, the bleached bones of an old wreck lay open like a flower to the late afternoon sun. Half buried in sand, it lay at rest, streamers of blackened seaweed trailing like tattered flags in the June air. Out in the loch a string of yachts sailed past some hazy islands, and the sky was streaked with the thinnest membrane of cloud.

A car roared into earshot, skidding to a halt by the quay. Charles was shouting, 'Nicky – I'm here' and leaping out. 'Oh, there you are. Right. Let's get cracking.' In seconds he had the hood up, and the ground littered with plastic bagfuls of gear: yellow oilies, a crate of beer, bits and pieces.

She got up. 'You're late.' She knew she sounded sulky.

'Sorry.' He ran to met her as she clambered up the quay steps. Flinging his arms round her, he kissed her. 'Oh you taste good. Have you seen the boat?' He was so eager, so passionate.

'Charles, let me go!' Nicky laughed, her body thrilled to be in contact with him, her mind remaining grouchy. 'I've been here, you know, since lunchtime.'

He carried her across the quay and dumped her at the edge like so much flotsam. Below lay a fishing boat *The Maid of Norway*, all gleaming varnished wood with green and gold on the gunwales. 'What d'you think then?'

'She's lovely, Charles.'

She's based on a traditional Norwegian design, did I tell you?' Charles stroked the wheelhouse door. 'Cost me a packet, I can tell you.'

'Have you tried her out?'

'Nope. They only delivered her yesterday – two weeks late. All the way from Bergen, via Scapa Flow.' He did a mock dance and whooped, 'Eat your heart out Miles old boy. Beat you to it!'

Miles was his partner in the surveying business Charles had taken over from his father, and the two of them had vied with each other over everything from the beginning, their cars, their houses – Miles had a mistress now, too.

'God, Nicky, I thought I'd never get away. Deirdre always finds something that *has* to be done at the last minute – the kids need their bikes fixed, to be taken to Gran's – this, or that. Every bloody Saturday. I told her I was getting the bloody boat organised for *her*, so we could all get away next weekend, but even that didn't stop her.'

'She is your wife. Maybe she senses – '

'Sense and Deirdre have never been known to connect, my darling. The kids and her damned patients are all she's interested in.' Charles leaped down onto the deck. 'Pass me the stuff, come on, snip snap.'

'Please, Charles, *please*. I'm *not* your wife, remember?' But, obediently enough, Nicky started handing bags down. 'What on earth have you got? This one weighs a ton.'

'Booze, some fruit, flares and whatever charts I could find. Jump. Oh come on, don't be afraid – I'm here to look after you.'

She scrambled down an ancient ladder into his arms.

'What's the big hurry?' The boat smelt of warm wood and new varnish, and his aftershave was familiar.

'We must reach West Loch Tarbert before nightfall.'

'Why?'

'Well, you know. I haven't actually sailed her before.

But Nicky's body was responding to contact with him. 'Charles, you can't be in *that* much of a hurry – we haven't seen each other for two whole weeks. Come below?'

He protested half-heartedly, but allowed her to pull him through the wheelhouse and down the short companionway into the cabin.

Later, the engine started first time. He was pleased. 'Perfect. God, is that the time?'

'What's the forecast?' she asked, sitting half in and half out of the wheelhouse to catch the last of the sun on her legs.

Charles pulled a jersey over his head. 'Well, darling, we – rather missed it, didn't we? Look at that sky. Set fair for days. Now, a beer. Fetch.'

'Fetch yourself. I want to steer.' She pushed him aside playfully.

'You've never been on a boat. D'you think I'm going to let you run this one onto the rocks? Oh all right. Keep her pointing over there, towards Jura. We don't want to be shipwrecked.' He did a Cossack leap through the cabin door to the fridge.

For the first time, Nicky found herself wondering how Deirdre coped with his moods. Normally he was like this, manically energetic, bright and cheerful, but sometimes, without warning, he would descend into a gloom so deep that neither drink nor sex would work and she would be forced to send him home.

Holding the wheel gave her an unexpected sense of power. They were nearing the mouth of the loch now, and the sea was no longer flat, rolling below them in slow curves. It was as if the boat were breathing gently, calmly. She found that a boat was more difficult to steer than a car, responding more slowly, liable to go too far – and you'd have travelled quite a distance before you were back on course.

The compass swung meaninglessly in its bath of glowing scarlet, above the chart table in front of her. 'Charles, how do you use this?'

He reappeared, squirting her with beer as he opened a can, licking droplets from her neck, taking over the wheel. 'You take a bearing, using the chart, and follow it. Look – ' he peered at the compass. 'That's odd. According to this we're heading North East. What the – ?'

'Well even I know that Jura is west of Crinan.'

'They can't have checked it. Damn. Just as well we'll make the West Loch before dark. Hey, if you hadn't tempted me, we'd have got away an hour ago – '

'Shut up. It was your fault,' she giggled.

Charles took the wheel again. 'Mmm. Let's hope everything else is working O.K. I mean, I told them I wanted a boat I could drive, with push-button controls. I don't have time to bone up on all that navigation stuff, and I'm not interested in the discomforts the yachties seem to enjoy. Any idiot should be able to work this. Let's have a bit of speed, now we're in open water.' He swung a lever and the engine responded. 'Fifteen knots. Good.'

'You're really thrilled with this, aren't you Charles?'

'Mmm. And it's just what I need for the new job – did I tell you we got it? Surveying most of the piers from here south – and it'll take most of the summer. They said this sort of boat was good on reliability, and there's all this room for the kids.'

'Yes.' She always hated when he brought his family into the conversation. She could cope with the dreadful-sounding Deirdre, providing he didn't go on about her for too long – but when he mentioned the children she felt too guilty for comfort.

'Weather forecast?' He clicked on the radio. 'At least this seems to be functional.'

'Ten to, yes, there should be one just about now.' She twiddled the knob till she found the station. ' . . . gale warning Irish Sea, Malin, Hebrides, force ten approaching rapidly. That's the end of the – '

He frowned. 'Drat. The clock's wrong. So – where's this gale then? The Met men never get it right.'

They drank their beer in silence, watching the green coast slip by on their left. Almost imperceptibly the thin cloud thickened till its greyness extinguished the blood-red wash of the sunset. A curtain of rain drew across Scarba, and the other islands faded from view. A hush came over the sea, followed by a shiver of little squalls, then the rain reached the boat, battering against the wheelhouse windows.

Nicky, mellowed with beer, watched Charles standing with negligent grace at the helm. His confidence, their lovemaking, and the warmth of the wheelhouse made her feel cosy, protected. She had been nervous about the sea, so black, so deep, so swirling with fearsome currents. Instead, she found she was enjoying the increasing surge and thrust of the swell rolling shoreward beneath them.

'These waves must have come all the way from America,' he said.

'Ireland, more likely.'

'Don't argue so much, Nicky. Here, take the helm then, for a while.'

'O.K.' Why was he restless, all of a sudden?

'This wind is getting up. I'd better do some checking. Hope these idiots filled her up. They don't seem to have done anything else I asked them to.' He went out on deck.

She tried unsuccessfully to stand upright, then she relaxed, going with the movement of the boat instead of fighting it. More strength was needed to hold the helm now. The rising wind was whisking the tops off the waves, and the fading light was making it increasingly difficult to see clearly.

The port and starboard lanterns came on, gleaming red and green eyes.

He came in, and went below. It was as if she and Charles were cocooned together in this wooden shell for ever. She wished it were true, that she were not merely the other woman. For three years, now, The Other Woman.

She no longer believed he'd leave Deirdre. So why didn't she tear herself away? Was this love – or mere addiction? What devil did she have within her that always made her want whatever was most difficult for her to get? It had been the same when she was a kid – falling out of trees trying to pick the apples nobody else dared to reach for, or perhaps were too sensible to want. What *did* she want out of life? Old-fashioned matrimony? Was that it? The great love scene, Gone With The Wind, the white wedding, the children, the whole shebang – like Charles and Deirdre? Wasn't that what all girls were supposed to dream about? So what was she doing messing about with a married man? She hadn't even got a proper career together – a bit of hotel work in summer, working as a chalet-girl during the Swiss winter season.

The boat fought for its freedom. What would happen if she let go the wheel? Elation flooded through her; she was riding some half-tamed sea stallion, its reins in her hands as they galloped in slow motion over endless hills. The storm was gathering force. She struggled to hold its head. She would not call for Charles.

A gust of wind together with a huge wave tipped the boat sideways. Beer cans, fruit and glasses hurtled across the wheelhouse, crashing on a wall. A hard object hit her on the side of the face. The next wave broke right over the boat, its full weight crashing against the windows. Still she held the helm steady, amazed that water should have this massive power. The boat heaved up, hung poised for a second, and thudded down on what felt like solid mud, but was in fact the huge bulk of another wave. She felt it would splinter into matchwood. 'Charles!'

Bending to look into the cabin, she was amazed to see him sitting with his head in his arms. Was he sea-sick?

'Whatever's wrong?' She thirled one part of her mind to the tortured seas, the increasing darkness, yelling, 'Come on up and help!'

'I can't.' His voice was petulant. 'It's no use. Nothing's working. There's not even any proper ballast.'

'What? How do you know?'

He shrugged.

'But she's just sailed across the North Sea, you said.'

'On the deck of a freighter.' His voice broke. 'Nicky, it's hopeless. There's hardly any diesel in the tank. I don't have a clue where we are. We've had it.'

'Charles, for goodness sake. We know we're between Scarba and Kintyre. I can't see far, but – tell me, do I stop the engine, or is it best to keep it going?'

'We're going to end up on the rocks.'

'Don't be so pathetic. Now, tell me what to do.'

From the corner of her eye she saw him roll on to a bunk, wailing, 'If I've got to die, I'm going to die down here.'

'Oh do me a favour. Don't be so melodramatic.' Disbelievingly she thought – this guy really has given up.

Blackness boxed her in. She could see nothing beyond the dimly lit, careening wheelhouse. She felt entombed, claustrophobic. What to do? Try to circle, stick around till daylight came? Using her scarf, she lashed the wheel as far to the right as she could. She had to escape, to free her mind to think.

Clinging to the door frame she clambered out. The wind felt solid, a giant hand trying to wipe her off the deck. Wet gusts whipped the hair around her face. The boat began to circle in the treacly sea, the white wake curling like a comet's tail, grinning at her – a widening smile, mocking.

'Always darkest before dawn,' she thought.

In spite of the wind, it was surprisingly quiet. The only sound came from the hissing spume. Muscular curves of ocean rolled by, spewing at her, bringing tears to her eyes. For some reason the African Queen came into her mind.

It had only been a story, but she remembered Katherine Hepburn's face, the jut of her jaw, the leeches, the mud, and her determination. This boat might go down, but she, Nicky, could swim, couldn't she? No coast could be that far away, could it?

Fear left her. The most basic animal instincts for survival took over. She'd never make the shore hampered by clothing. She began to strip off, tossing jeans, sodden jersey, bra and briefs into the wheelhouse. A plastic bag caught her eye. The flares. Well, it was worth a try. Taking advantage of the next wave, she lurched inside. The bag had slid into a corner, but the flares were still dry. The cabin light gave out just as she finished reading the instructions.

Out on deck again, her legs braced each side of the doorway, she pulled a trigger. Seconds later the sky glowed fluorescent pink. She fired off three of them. The last she'd keep till later. Now there was nothing to do but wait.

Weaving her fingers into the safety rope on the wheelhouse roof, her feet spreadeagled, clinging to the deckboards, a sense of exhileration took over. Her fate was now in the hands of others until such time as she decided to swim for it. She was at one with the boat, the ocean, the storm, freed from the trappings and trivia of civilisation. Only she and the elements existed. She laughed out loud into the storm. This freedom just to be, to feel, was wonderful, whether she were to live or to die.

Charles? Suddenly she realised she hadn't given him a thought. How irrelevant he was to her life.

The engine puttered into silence. The wake died and the boat's movement changed to a sickening wallow. But a luminousness was beginning to show through the rain. As Nicky's clinging fingers chilled into claws, the sea's colour changed from black to grey. Dawn was coming.

The sound of an engine thrummed into her consciousness. Out of the rain, a dark blue and orange shape became a lifeboat. Nicky's shouts were snatched away by the wind. Then she was yelling, 'Charles, they're here. You're going to be O.K.'

The lifeboat was perilously near. How would they not collide? A man in yellow oilskins called to her. A rope snaked through the downpour. She missed it. He tried again. This time she grabbed it. What to tie it to? She found a bollard at the stern, her stiff fingers barely remembering a reef knot. The boats heaved up and down almost in synchrony now, separated only by squawking fenders. A lifeboatman came aboard and made fast another rope. 'Any injured?' he enquired, apparently blind to her nakedness, his eyes roving everywhere else on the deck. 'The Coastguard saw your flares.'

Experiencing a wash of relief that threatened to make her legs buckle under her, she said 'There's a man. Down there,' pointing. Then she was being lifted up. 'A mermaid for you, Doctor. She'll need a blanket,' and she was passed over the side into the lifeboat.

Soon she was swaddled in respectable blankets, sipping tea in the warm cabin. Only when the men were questioning her, praising her for her decision to circle, her attempt to stay in the same area, did her teeth start chittering, her whole body one great rigor of shakes and shock. She watched, in a detached way, as they brought Charles in. He was limp and sleepy. The doctor examined them both while the crew radioed the Coastguard.

As the lifeboat purred towards Oban, Nicky knew she was free at last. She felt only normal human pity for Charles hunched in his blanket, gazing into space. His beautiful boat had been left as so much flotsam, perhaps to be salvaged, perhaps to sink. He didn't need her to wreck his family too. From now on she'd steer her own course, openly. No more drifting about, clinging to whatever passed her way.

# *A GIRL'S BEST FRIEND*

DRIPS PLONKED onto the soggy floor of the dungeon.

'Gosh,' said Zenobia, one hand deep in a fissure, 'They're still here!' She pulled something out and thrust it at Marcia.

'Ugh, you clot, it's all slimy!' Marcia dropped the package. The torch wobbled golden circles over the cracked rock, which oozed shiny green pus and breathed an earthen odour like Kelvinbridge underground at home.

We scanned the sludge beneath our wellies and Zenobia found the small bundle of mouldy newspaper. She crouched down and pulled it apart.

Rainbow reflections scattered over the tunnel walls as though from some glitterball at a dance.

'You'd never think such a small handful of diamonds could throw so much light,' I said.

'Oh shut up, Smells, that's exactly wot you said wen we planted them.' Marcia was still so bloody English,you never got an 'h' in what, when, where or why. For some reason she was O.K. on who.

My name is, unfortunately, Esmeralda. I'm the only one of the Musketeers whose nickname still sticks from the time

when, twenty-five years ago, the three of us were all at this
boarding-school. We lived in a converted house next to a
castle in Fife. Marcia used to have long golden hair and look
like a Vestal Virgin. The staff always believed everything she
said, so she was used as our Front.

Zen held the diamonds up as if they were holy relics.
'Gosh, quarter of a century? And no-one's discovered them.
Poor thingies. Poor Stefano.' The five-row choker dripped
from her hand like a petrified waterfall. You could tell she
was nearly crying. Reaching up, she began to put it round
her neck.

Marcia practically snatched it out of her hands. 'Give it
to me, Zen. We *were* always sure they were paste anyway,
weren't we?' She held it up to the light. 'I'll take care of it.
You always use to lose everything.' She smiled.

Zen's grin spilt her face like a gleeful turnip lantern. Her
bone-structure had sunk without trace long ago. 'Cripes, all,
wait till we tell everyone in Sally's!'

'Wot on earth do you mean? We can't possibly tell.
There'd be the most God-awful scandal. Anyway it might not
be – safe.'

I knew what Marcia meant.

Here we all were, among two thousand respectable
matrons and other pillars, assembled like battery hens in the
University hostels during its off-season to celebrate the
centenary of our Old School. It was 1975 and a lot of water
had passed under all our bridges, not to mention other
flotsam and jetsam.

Marcia's hair had gone fawn, crimped and tortured into
the style she thought suitable to a vicar's widow living in
provincial Essex. She and I had persuaded Zenobia to come
with us for the frolic. Yesterday everyone had been stiff and
formal, stalking about still mentally clad in the minks,
Bentleys and nannies of home, or the blue-stockings of
academic stardom. But after last night's bash all shreds of
dignity had gone to pot. Magically – thanks to many large

gins – we became again the gels we had been. And the feeling had lasted right through church today. Even the choirboys looked the same as they used to. We were dizzy with youth and irresponsibility.

The same seemed to have happened to all the other age-groups. Bunches of neo-gels, from octogenarians to those still in their dewy twenties, had swaggered round the school slapping each other on the back, reminiscing and recognising slogans still visible on the ancient desks alongside more modern stuff like 'Miss Murgatroyd is gay', which would have been considered a revolting example of sucking-up in our day.

In our day Marcia, Zenobia and I had wrapped the diamond choker carefully in a sherbet-shandy bag, then in a copy of the St Andrew's *Herald*. Sweating with fear and horror and excitement, we'd scaled the castle walls. For the usual fee, old Groper had let us borrow the key to the dungeon. Old Groper was the custodian who did Saturday evening shifts in summer. He knew us well. In return for a wee kiss – which included a bit of body contact – Marcia's bum, my thick thigh, or Zen's lesser bosom (she liked to keep her best one for Stefano) Groper would let us into the grounds.

It was there we met any boyfriends we could sufficiently interest. Mine was usually an acne-ridden choirboy called Norman. We exchanged passionately meaningful looks all through Sunday sermons and had an elaborate system of notes left in an arrow-slit of the castle wall.

Marcia was actually keener on the junior gymn mistress but put up with one of Norman's mates for decency's sake. Zen was really mature. She slept regularly with Stefano, an Italian medical student from a hostel which was conveniently just across the road from our House. A useful shrubbery lay against the wall in our grounds, providing cover for her weekly excursions.

Occasionally he'd meet all three of us there before

smuggling Zen up the fire-escape to his room. Being Italian he was very passionate, she used to explain. Apparently you couldn't control a man like that, it was bad for him. So you had to Give In. Zenobia's education came to an end when she got expelled for being engaged to Stefano – and pregnant.

Now she was on her third marriage, having converted to the Jewish religion. Stefano and Catholicism hadn't worked out. After he got done in by his godfather or someone, she had decided to make a change. She'd left a trail of six children before landing back in Edinburgh with this jeweller. She was quite happy, because Something-stein (I can never remember his name – a little grey-rabbit man) turned an aged and blind eye to her weekly infidelities. She had as much rope as she could use and a good house in the New Town.

Compared to Zenobia and Marcia, my life was textbook suburbia. Children – a boy and a girl and heterosexual so far as one could judge, who only occasionally irritated their father, my husband. He's a workaholic GP. I play golf and work the antique markets. Edwardian jewellery mostly, though I'll try anything I can carry. I want to have a shop of my own.

Marcia runs a business full-time. It must be pretty healthy though she won't talk about it, because she drives this Ferrari and wears silver mink to balls. Not like most vicar's widows. But her stepson's on heroin.

It had been because of Zenobia that we got the diamond choker.

We'd found it in the bootroom one Saturday, while we were changing for Games. Our school was modelled on Eton, so we had enforced Games every day including Saturdays to mould our characters. It was in Marcia's hockey boot. She stubbed her chilblain on it. While she was screaming in agony I read the note.

'This piccolo gift I offer you for your quiet. S.'

'Of course they're only paste,' Marcia had said. 'But jolly dee. Woolworth's, wot?' Just because it was her boot she assumed they were exclusively for her.

I had pointed out that I, too, had to be kept quiet – and that if it hadn't been for dear old Zenobia we wouldn't have anything to be quiet about – so the choker belonged to all three of us. At that age I was still naively trying to live up to the Christian Ethic instilled into me every holidays by my father.

The problem was what to do with the diamonds. We couldn't very well wear them. Flash was forbidden in any form, even sleepers. Our things were meticulously inspected every Sunday – each drawer, bag and desk gone through. Everyone was a suspect till proved innocent, even the prefects. You couldn't hide a stick of Wrigley's or a dirty sock with any hope of success.

Shivering along the road back to our House after hockey (I'd been in goal again – two hours of hypothermia as punishment for running in some corridor), I suggested the tunnel. I read a lot of Enid Blyton. We knew there was one running from a dungeon, and the public weren't allowed in. We would have no problem, with Old Groper's help.

We called in to see him and arranged everything. Marcia, who lied like an angel, convinced him we were researching the Past of some bishop who got martyred there. He swallowed it whole.

About a week after the *fait* was *accompli*, the Mafia theft was even splashing the headlines of the quality press we were permitted to peruse. Interpol were hunting for the killer of some Italian countess *and* for a diamond choker she'd been wearing to a charity ball in London. I still have the photo I cut out.

Apparently this countess had been on the Mafia's black list for years, having fled to Britain for sanctuary. Her dismembered body still in bits of ballgown had been collected from the branches of trees in Hyde Park. But a section of her neck was missing – and the choker.

Zenobia nudged me back to the present. 'Cripes all, what

are we going to do with the lovely thing? It's – well – a bit of an embarrassment really, isn't it? Remember all the hoo ha?'

'Wy don't I take it south to a little man I know in Bond Street?' Marcia slipped the choker into her pocket, extinguishing its fire.

'I say, come to that, my beloved could tell us if they're real or not.' Zenobia bent, darkening the oval pool of light.

I grabbed the torch from Marcia. 'Shsh, someone's coming. Listen.' I shoved her against the wall and in the confusion dropped it. The plastic shattered on a jut of rock and tinkled, lightless, into the sludge.

'Oh Smells,' giggled Zenobia, 'you clot! Now we can't see.'

In the darkness the earth-odour seemed stronger and the drips louder, echoing round the dungeon behind us. I used to wonder if one wasn't rather too near Hell, when I Believed.

'Marcia, feel along the wall with one hand, and hold on to Zenobia's back with the other.' I snaked forward.

'Wear are you Zen?' Marcia's voice was going high. 'Witch way's the dungeon? Oh Zen, I'm scared.'

Already I'd found the dungeon corner. For an instant I hesitated. There was the feel of someone else being there, in the dark. My eyes were getting better at seeing through the blackness. Where I thought the ladder led up from the dungeon there seemed to be a paler gloom. Then the whispers started. Sibilant sound wound round the chamber, elusive as smoke. I remembered its facility for behaving like a whispering gallery.

I made for the dimness at the foot of the ladder, quite confident, now, of my direction. There was a waft of *Muguet de Bois* talc, and my face was buried in a soft body. It gave a sharp intake of breath. The thick tweed was neither Zenobia nor Marcia. Then the breath came out in jerks, exhaling as giggles. 'Let go my coat, idiot! Jilly, let me go! Oh help!' Voice rising in fear, 'Who – who is it?' A hand gropes my face. 'No specs – you're not Peter –'

Clearly we were neither the first nor the last schoolgirls to make use of the castle. There was no way of knowing how many of them were in the dungeon with me, and I thanked God for the confusion that ensued. My hand found the ladder, as I heard old girls and new girls meeting in gales of mirth.

The mini was quite discreetly parked beneath the overgrown bushes of the shrubbery over the wall. By the time the girls sorted themselves out, I'd be half-way to Glasgow.

The diamonds rattled merrily in my hand. Not bad for an amateur pickpocket, I thought. There would be no difficulty disposing of them through the underground. I knew a little Italian family. They had an icecream shop near Kelvinbridge.

It would be just right for my antique jewellery business. I'd buy it from them. And continue to work for the underground. Like Marcia, I knew the diamonds were real.

# *SNOWBALLS IN SUMMER*

ONE HOT SUMMER not so long ago an artist called Andy Goldsworthy filled the generously proportion-ed exhibition space of the Tramway Theatre in Glasgow with his collection of giant snowballs.

He made them the winter before in the far north and transported them by refrigerated lorry to a deep freeze in the fish-market, keeping them till now for us to enjoy. Each one measures about three feet high and they are laid out on the plain concrete floor in two neat rows, several yards of space between each, peppermint white, fresh and cool.

Outside, the temperature rises to 75 degrees Fahrenheit.

After the official opening, the public begin to drift in for a look. Some have come out of sheer curiosity, others to show how open-minded they are, or to have their prejudices confirmed. Responses range from quiet murmurs of approval to blank incomprehension: 'Well, I may not know much about art, but I know what I like and I don't like this – Couldn't put these in your living-room – why don't they do *nice* things any more? – This one looks like a bunch of old car parts – Could have thought it up myself on a wet day – Think what it must have cost – And you can't even sell them, they'll just melt – You don't need a college degree to make snowballs.'

Why do we have such fixed ideas about what Art is?

Of course we women, living and working in the last decade of the twentieth century, have a lot to do. We do not have a great deal of spare time for gazing at the wilder and more incomprehensible extravances of the Arty crowd, let alone a bunch of old snowballs. But maybe we should pay a little more heed to what our contemporaries are trying to say through their various Arts – we may learn something to our advantage. As women, we account for over 50% of the population, yet how many of us take a regular day off in the week? A day of free time that is, not a day to do the housework but one in which we can please ourselves utterly – a day to stand and stare at the world we inhabit – a day in which to think.

The viewers chatter on; 'A child of six could have made them – So, what's the point? – Load of rubbish – Who do they think they're kidding – A pure con.'

The snowballs don't argue. As the days go by they melt slowly, silently, weeping rings of silent drips into growing pools of tranquil reflection.

As their substance dissipates, each reveals its true nature in a different way. Some are simply made of snow. Others have secrets to divulge. One is brown, stuffed full of pine needles like a giant truffle, another spotted with flat grey stones – the kind that make good skimmers on summer days by the sea. One is translucent gold, filled with deep-frozen daffodils picked in Spring and perfectly preserved till now.

Some of us pop in again to see how the meek and silent snowballs are faring, conscious, somehow, of their disintegration – of watching something die, and the associated melancholic atmosphere of the surrounding space.

As the plain ones melt, their water content trickles away to disappear down the nearest drain. The heat of the day dries up the residual wetness so that not a trace of their existence remains. When the snow has gone from the truffle-ball, a crown of thorns is left on the concrete for our consideration, a perfect circle of bristles. The flat stones have formed a miniature pebble beach reflected in their own little sea. The yellow snowball is gently dropping daffodils, one by one, to make a green and yellow garland for its dying hours.

Each of us is 75% water, rolled up with a little skin, bone, gristle, fat, hair, D.N.A. 'We are what we eat' some say – but it's not about food, an apple a day, wholemeal bread. We're very good at knowing all about physical fitness – it's better for our bodies to be fed wholefoods. Brown bread may taste strange after years of Mother's Pride, but after a while we begin to enjoy the richer taste and texture, start to say it's the best thing since sliced bread. After the conversion, bleached white seems tasteless.

Why should our minds be different? For surely our minds are equally the product of what we consume?

How can we get more roughage into our mental diet? One of the first requirements, if we want to nourish our minds, is free time. We must demand – and see that we take – the right to time of our own on a regular basis, no matter whether it's from a job, the baby, the aged parent or the handicapped dependant. The shorter the time we have, the greater the necessity to use it well, not to squander it on trivia.

We should treat our minds, when they're off duty, with at least as much care as we do our bodies, opening them to ideas that are more interesting, more challenging than a surfeit of ice-cream romance, pretty pictures, sloppy songs. That is not to say that there are not times when nothing but sweetness and ease can help us through a difficult slice of life. But our minds need training, toning up, exercise as well as relaxation, if our 50% of the human race is reach its full potential in the world.

Consider becoming a snowball. Not one which rolls passively around gathering no moss and which, when you die, will leave nothing but a puff of vapour behind, but one in whose design you take an active part, so that it becomes stuffed full of interesting things.

Too many of the women of history have simply melted away leaving no trace, except for the odd queen, a nurse or two, one Prime Minister, the odd scientist, and a handful of Suffragettes. If we are not to follow them into oblivion, we have to make more effort than we do at present.

What has all this to do with attitudes to contemporary Art? It's about waking up to what is going on now. Pictures which match the carpet become part of the wallpaper, requiring no further thought. They're not harmful, just empty. Buying these, looking at them in your spare time, is simply a waste of that time – and your money.

One reason we are so illiterate where the Arts are concerned is because we are woefully under-educated in that area. Unless we stop the present lunge towards pragmatism in schools, blindly vocational training in colleges, the situation will get worse. No amount of number-crunching will prise open the psyche, awaken it to the possibility of change-for-the-better.

All art forms are communications. Risk allowing what they communicate to disturb you, to make your mind creak into some sort of response. You the viewer, the listener, the reader, are required to participate – and not necessarily in words. The process is dangerous – you may be hit in the eye with an uncomfortable contemporary issue you'd rather dodge, and thus forced to confront it, to consider it, maybe even *do* something about it. Listening to more demanding music or poetry, looking at abstract art, you don't *have* to 'understand', only to keep your mind open, savour sounds, textures, colours, images, feel the mood, the concerns of the piece, allow it to connect with you. Be disappointed if you come out from seeing a new play *without* questions and ideas reverberating in your mind.

If we are only what we eat, then rubbish is all we can become.

Because we *are* capable of thinking, dreaming, loving, we have the potential of being more than that. Adding up to at least 50% of the human race, of the population of each nation, each district, each town, each community, each street, we *can* start to change the world – we *can* leave more behind us than a trail of empty statistics.

The Tramway is empty now, all the physical evidence of Andy Goldsworthy's snowballs gone. The viewers were right when they noted there would be nothing to sell. It is true that children of six can make them. There isn't much to understand about a snowball, is there? So why is it that, years later, I am left with a clear image of these innocent objects, my definition of Art challenged, my imagination stretched beyond articulacy? For they exist, still, in my mind, the thoughts and ideas generated by them burning on in my brain, a light rekindled by so many things – by pine needles, by daffodils, by a child of six weeping in the street.

# LANDSCAPE WITH STILL LIFE

A SHIVER OF WIND rattles the rowan tree, shaking it so that leaves fall in a scarlet shower upon the Artist. She is framed in the double 'O' of my binoculars, her yellow hair tied in a knot on top of her little head, innocent-looking fronds escaping above the red silk scarf. Her shoulders appear vulnerable in the over-large terra cotta-coloured artist's smock. She is well-camouflaged indeed against the raging late-September sunset.

One dead leaf lands on her canvas and sticks to the wet red paint. With fastidious fingers she attempts to lift it off, but her touch crumbles it to dust. She looks up, perhaps to see if another squall threatens, but the rowan is almost bare now except for its crop of blood berries, left for the hungry beaks of winter birds.

She is painting an Autumn landscape today, in oils. Rich sweeps of Burnt Siena, Crimson Lake, Ochre and Carmine curve across her canvas, expressing rather than mimicking her Renfrewshire view.

I shift a little on my stomach. Birdwatching is a damp

pastime. But now, just before dusk, the greylag come skeining in across the dull sky, circle once, then slant down to land with a whirr of wings, their awkward undercarriages splayed out, webbed feet feeling for the ploughed earth. Movement is followed by a hushed pause as the birds settle their feathers. Such innocent creatures, geese, every year returning to the same fields in the east-facing fold of the hill. They have been coming, generation on generation, for hundreds of centuries. They still arrive, though now men shoot them.

The Artist notes the change they make to the colour of her landscape. She mixes paint then smears their grey blur over her Red Umber field. At dusk the hunters will come in their green boots, their khaki war-like Barbour-jackets, golden labrador bitches running at their heels.

I watch her. Slightly distorted by the telephoto effect of my binoculars, she is utterly recognisable. A double ring of rainbows surround her from the prisms. I wonder if that is how he sees her, suffused, as it were, with a more than ordinary glory.

'You have to be determined if you want to be a painter,' she's always said. 'Dedicated. Everything else must take second place, even friends. The Art must always come first.'

She has proved correct. I remember how during our school years she always took the art prizes, had her childish pictures hung in local exhibitions. At Art College in the sixties she worked all the time, until the natural light faded at the windows. The rest of us played at being cool, man, experimenting with sex thanks to the new Pill, and drugs thanks to Hippy ideals of freedom, wearing beads and flowers as emblems of love and goodwill.

I never draw, now. I teach in a battered downtown Comprehensive. Her work fetches thousands. Galleries in London fall over themselves to get hold of her work, rumour says she more or less named her price for the contract with the New York connection. Examples of her art hang in the public collections of capital cities the world over.

I am forgotten.

Soft bootfalls slop through the marsh behind me. I hear the dogs' whiffling breaths. The hunters have arrived. They will lie a while, waiting for twilight, then the shooting will begin. He will be among them, he never misses the geese.

I feel the gun by my side. It's loaded and ready. The shot that kills her will just be one among many, un-noticeable among the other shots. Like a firing-squad. And when they find her, they'll think it was an accident. It will be an extra touch of irony if they think he killed her.

For it is certain that he will have boasted about her to his shooting mates. He has probably enjoyed being seen with her, a new toy, better than the Mackintosh, faster than any Porsche – with greater risks attached. Maybe some of them even think she's his wife, for his new cronies don't know about me.

I am the cast-off, the old wife, shed like a chrysalis for the new image. For ten years I have watched, quietly and with apparent docility, his antics with these child-women. I have stayed in the sham home, acted out my role as part of a pretend couple till the very core of my nature has festered and rotted. It will be worth spending the rest of my ruined life in a cell to have had this one moment of triumph, to be rid of just one of these sores, the most recent, the most dangerous, this fair, free Artist.

The sun has set. She paints faster now, in a hurry no doubt to finish her work before dark, like me. Tubes of paint lie scattered at her feet, glinting gunmetal grey in the bracken.

The hunters writhe nearer through the brushwood behind me. They think they are silent but I hear them. The stench of damp, decaying leaves rises from the earth and a silent fog sweats from the rushes to swirl in little whorls around the tussocks of bog-grass.

What if the months of target-practice fail me? Failure has dogged me all my life, why should I now expect to succeed?

Like a mist seeping into my mind a different plan begins to form. Why not let her live?

What if I give him the divorce he craves? He will feel forced to marry her, to take her on. She will be obliged to go through with their charade, no escape, no excuses once the path is cleared. Let her live on, condemned to spend the rest of her life with him and all his little meannesses, his incapabilities, his infidelity?

And I, free for ever of the constant humiliation, free to watch her suffer as I have suffered, to see her squirm at parties, peel his fat hands from greedy bosoms, fold his wilting drink-sodden body into dark limousines at dead of night?

A shot rings out. Geese rise in an arc against the blood-red sky. The Artist falls to the ground, spurting small scarlet fountains. A man shouts. The Artist is surrounded by men and dogs. Disembodied voices calling to each other, 'She's not – is she?' 'I'm afraid so' mingle with 'Heel Delilah', 'Leave that alone, girl'.

The geese fly up, a cloud of innocent grey ghosts, darkening to a black vee-formation up and away to the south-west.

The men grunt. They are picking her up, taking her away. Not 'her' any longer. A body has no gender, the Artist has become 'it'. A car engine roars, and they are gone.

All is silent but for the seepings of the bog, the tricklings of ditch-water.

I unload my gun. I am innocent, free now to untie the bonds of bitterness. Perhaps he truly loved this Artist, after all. He too will feel pain. What purpose would there have been in revenge? I can find a better way to end my days than in some solitary cell, these foetid classrooms.

The landscape lies completed, face-down in the mud, forgotten. I use it as a stepping-stone, pressing it down on my way past.

# *WHEN WINTER COMES*

THE GATE, mossed and cracked over old white paint, stands slightly open, a finger of September sunshine pointing into the gloom beyond.

'Inviting,' says my father, his brown eyes twinkling small-boy mischief from their eighty-nine-year-old sockets.

'Someone might be there,' I hang back, reluctant, unwilling to trespass.

From beyond the tangle of overgrown bushes, thorns, nettles and flowers, a seagull squawks derisively. We can still hear the waves of the firth breaking on the shore behind us.

While I hesitate, my father, bent double, head down, squeezes himself through the narrow gap and treads purposefully up the weedy, red-gravelled drive. But he doesn't get very far because the bushes have been growing unchecked for years and now look like the barrier of thorns around Sleeping Beauty's castle. Now he is bulldozing his way through, dwarfed by the fankle of dead brown branches.

Above, against the blue of the sky, a bower of shining veridian-green escallonia and rhododendron flourishes, unpruned and uninhibited.

I am a respectable middle-aged woman. I can't possibly trespass. 'Dad' I shout. 'Come out. There might be somone...'

He is genuinely a little deaf, but plays on this selectively. Clearly he does not wish to hear me. He has now disappeared into the undergrowth beyond the first curve in the driveway.

The estate once belonged to an heirless ancestor of ours, the last of that particular line of the family – it must be forty years since I was last there, an awkward girl, shy of the Edwardian aunts in their lace collars, nerves rattling my teacup in its dainty saucer, terrified I would disgrace myself in some unimaginable way, the uncle all tweed and gun-dogs, puffing a pipe in his gruff bachelorhood.

My father's voice comes through the bushes, 'Uncle Bill always kept the place so immaculate. Fifteen farms, he owned.' Always impressed by worldly success.

Reasoning that I might never have the chance again to indulge an old man's whim, I glance quickly over my shoulder to see if anyone is looking, then hurriedly slide through the gateway and plunge into a twilight zone. Branches tear at my hair, briars scratch my face as I push ahead, trying to catch up with him.

I can hear him forging ahead steadily, his footfalls crunching dead twigs, apparently oblivious of the thickening tangle, intrepid. His skin must be made of leather.

He has this quality of dogged determination: I can imagine him climbing Himalayan mountains, or rowing over huge waves – the Old Man of the Sea – or tramping across snowy wastes like Scott of the Antarctic. As my father he has always seemed monumental, somehow, though his physique is slim.

When next I see him he is in the clear, outlined in a pool of sunlight on what had once been the lawn, the remains of his hair a white halo lifted a little by an eddy of air, his face in shadow. He points.

At his feet lie a painting, stained by damp although the glass is still intact, a book, glossy pages wavy with rainwater, and a corroded trombone with a battered end. 'Vandals, or burglars.' I say. 'They can't leave a place alone, can they?'

'They used to give these wonderful parties . . .' my father's gaze drifts towards the house-front. 'We would dance till dawn. Then we'd swim down at the shore there.' Rusting pillars support a shallow iron veranda which still shows traces of green paint. There isn't a pane of glass that hasn't been broken. Green paint flakes from rotting astrakals and one half of the French windows hangs half off its hinges, creaking back and forth, back and forth in the light wind. 'That was the drawing room – do you remember?'

'Not really, Dad.' You can't share every memory – you weren't there, you weren't part of that time of life, it's hard to imagine. 'All I remember is darkness, warmth, brown wood, smokiness, these wet labradors wagging their tails, or spread out to dry by the fire.'

He is looking in at the next window along. 'That was the library'.

I join him, peering in. A few damp and mouldering tomes are still stuck to the shelves with cobwebs. The rest have been flung all over the floor, spilled out into the garden at our feet – I can feel them beneath the grass. I wonder what else is buried there.

His voice has an edge of anger. 'You'd think someone would have bought the place – it's just been left to rot.'

The whole village had belonged to the estate. When Uncle Bill died – oh all of ten years ago – it had been bought over lock, stock and barrel for the land by some insurance company. The cottages had been sold off one by one at inflated prices to commuters wealthy enough to own fast cars that would get them to town inside an hour, people powerful enough so that it didn't matter if they weren't in the office by nine. Why had no-one wanted this, the Big House, with its Edwardian veranda, its secluded position, its character? Its aura is not unpleasant, it is large, but not vast, and it must have a marvellous view, from the top storey at least, over the bushes to the river.

'I first met your mother on this lawn,' my father smiles at me, testing to see if I'm bored by his nostalgia.

'Tell me about it,' I encourage him.

'She was standing where you are, in the moonlight. She was late – her little red tourer had broken down on the way.' He laughed. 'It was always breaking down, that car. She was wearing a dress made of glittery beads and she just stood there – well – shining. She was the most beautiful woman I had ever seen, you know.' He isn't sad, he's enjoying the memory. 'Her hands were black with oil and she had to go and wash. We danced all night, then I followed her home. Her car conked out on every hill – and I pushed it with the bumper of my bull-nose Morris, till we reached the top.'

He is off again, stomping through the grass round the side of the house. A gutter hangs at an angle, rusting lace netting veils a rectangle that was clearly once a tennis-court. He stumbles a little, his foot turning up a bald and greening ball from a tussock. 'They gave wonderful tennis parties in summer. Everyone came, there were cars all down the drive. Afterwards we would have tea on the veranda. Your mother was a fine player.'

She's dead many a long year – gone long before her time, fading away to transparency and then to nothingness. What kind of a young man had he been when she met him? You can't think of your father as a youth – perhaps because it was before your own time. His stories, memories, old photographs form a family mythology as familiar as fairy-tales, known since ever you could listen to words and understand their meaning.

'It was such a lively place.' He is sad, now. 'What a waste to let it go like this.'

'Oh, someone will buy it, Dad. Maybe they already have

– and they just haven't started work on it yet – it's too nice a place not to– ' My attempt at comfort sounds hollow, false.

'The arty crowd used to come down here for weekends, to paint, and write poetry. Your mother sang – I was never any good at that sort of thing. There were some odd characters. Bohemians, we used to call them. They wore those floppy ties, you know.' Does he wish he'd been wild and free, unconventional, an artist? Evening meanderings on our old piano had been this plain-suited businessman's private passion, *Humoresque* his signature-tune. Does he feel his age? He never talks about it, never complains. If he's ill he covers up, not wanting to seem weak. We have orders not to visit him if he's ever taken to hospital – he wants everyone to remember him on his feet. So far he's only ever landed up in hospital because of some accident – the time he broke his neck falling down Buchaille Etive Mhor one New Year's day, the time he fell off the roof of our island cottage, the time he fell between the train and the station, in too much of a hurry to get to work. He had survived all these, but permanently damaged, and he could no longer walk his beloved hills.

The sun warms my back. The old garden is sheltered from the main blast of the wind, secret, peaceful, the smoke from a log-fire or a bonfire from one of the cottages wafting gently around. He doesn't want to be cremated. It is to be my task to see that he is buried in the ground, like his ancestors.

'Fed up with being old, Dad?'

'Not much you can do about it, dear.' He looks around. 'But I don't like waste.' This place is depressing him. He picks up the trombone, a small boy, curious. Worms squiggle away from beneath it. He drops it. 'The musical evenings they had. Your mother and I used to sing – Scottish songs – the Kennedy-Frasers.'

He turns over the painting – 'It's just a print' – and lifts the book. It has been lying on a stone and is remarkably dry. 'Robert Louis Stevenson. I'll keep this. *The Master of Ballantrae*. I read all these books when I was a boy.

Stevenson's father was an engineer with the lighthouses, you know.' He tucks it into his jacket.

A rhythmic thumping comes from the other side of the house, a crashing in the woods, a dog barks and a woman's voice shouts a curse. Into the sunlight trots a bright chestnut horse, its head high, nostrils flaring, the rider looking over her shoulder at a black labrador following her.

Embarrassed again, an intruder, a trespasser, I take my father's hand. I wait for the woman to see us, for her to tell us to get off her land.

The dog snuffs round the trombone then bounds towards us. I wait for her anger.

'Get down, Bruce,' she shouts at the dog. 'Heel, boy.' Then she just nods and says 'Hi' absently, and trots on past the tennis court. She is a trespasser too, using the dereliction of the garden for her riding-ground.

I pull my father towards the dark tangle of the driveway whence we came. 'Come on, Dad.' Brambles catch in my hair, the berries shining black, almost out of reach. They are fat and full of juice. I pick one and pop it into his mouth.

He finds a late raspberry and offers it to me. 'They've grown wild and small, but tasty enough all the same.'

We are cramming our mouths with fruit and laughing like naughty children, the juice running down our chins, our hands stained red and purple.

'How on earth are we going to get out of here?' I ask.

'Backwards,' he says, showing me how, bending stiffly and presenting the back of his thickly padded jacket to the thorns, pushing through steadily, hunch-backed, his head patiently lowered as if he was an old horse sheltering from the weather. He has always shown me how, with kindness and warmth, only angry when I was an impossible teenager, or when the ideals of our different eras clashed, his having told him to protect his wife and child, to aim for dull security, mine insisting on freedom and equality.

I follow in his wake, breaking off stems and branches –

rhododendron, escallonia, rose-hips.

Breathless, we emerge by the gate. 'A bouquet of cuttings for you, and some seeds.' Bowing, I present him with my pickings. 'To remind you of today, and yesterday, and to preserve a bit of Uncle Bill's garden for posterity. You can grow them on, for next Spring. You'll be ninety next Spring – imagine.' Will he last another winter? Last year the flu so nearly turned to pneumonia.

He creaks upright, rubbing his back ruefully, eyes twinkling. Inside he's not an old man, but a mischievous boy again. We slide guiltily round the stuck gate, partners in crime. A passer-by stares. We fetch our picnic from the car boot and take it down to the rocks, staring out across the shining river.

# LADIES' DAY

IRIS TOOK OFF her skirt and jumper and hung them neatly on the wire coat-hanger. The chlorine smell reached even into this comfortable inner sanctum of the baths. She smoothed the satin slip over her hips – French navy, very modern – conscious of her warm body odour wafting upwards. She was glad of the flowered curtain that hid her from the eyes of the two ladies wrapped in towels sitting in the armchairs beyond. She was feeling a little shy, being the New Girl.

New Girl. What nonsense, at forty-nine. Not much new about that. But her new life was beginning, and she couldn't expect it to be altogether a comfortable experience. The loneliness was the worst, so far. She did miss Mother.

The ladies were talking. 'That's what I like about the club – it's so clean. Dick has turned out to be a good choice, don't you think Claire?'

'Mmm. Though some of the Young wanted a woman coach, for once. Staying for tea afterwards?'

'Oh yes, for once dear. There are times when only one's female friends will do. That awful plumber! I want a good long moan, over chocolate eclairs and Lapsang Souchong.'

Iris was intrigued. Might Gert reveal more if she stayed hidden in her cubicle?

'O.K. for you, old girl, thin as a pin and fit as a fiddle.'

'Give up the weed, Claire, give up the weed.'

Once she got to know the set-up it would be fine, thought Iris, it was just the beginning that was a little – tricky. Ladies' Days were such a pleasure after school, Josie had said, specially in wet November. It was Josie who had persuaded her to join. They were to take swimming lessons at 4 p.m. each Ladies' Day – Tuesdays and Thursdays – because now she needed something to look forward to after school. There had to be more to life than school, and the girls bored and up to their tricks, like that Smith character with her cheeky grin. Funny how children nowadays weren't really interested in Biology – she'd always found it fascinating.

Carefully she unhooked her all-in-one Marks & Sparks firm- control at the crotch – matching undies, all the rage – what luxury. She rolled down the navy tights and peeled off the lacy briefs – very daring, what would Mother have said? She hung them on the coat-hanger so that they were secreted discreetly behind the folds of her pleated skirt. Mother had always favoured sensible cotton. They had wrapped her in her cotton shroud only a month ago, though it seemed like years. A different life must be organised now, after all the worry. Poor Mother, she had never wanted to be difficult.

She stepped into the new swim-suit – navy blue with pink flowers and the legs not cut too high. Her forty-nine year old breasts swung down as she bent, like little sacks of liquid, though hers had never 'given suck' as Shakespeare would have it. She'd long ago given up wondering what that felt like. The bra-cups were stiff enough to hide your shape quite well.

From the security of her flowery cubicle, she heard someone else enter the room. Josie: 'Oh, hullo, Gert. Is my friend here yet?'

Iris swished back the curtain, pulling in her tummy, feeling as revealed as Miss World. 'What do we do with our bags?'

The armchairs, placed in rows along each wall, were draped with white sheets. A line of low tables supported ashtrays, magazines and newspapers, and at one end lay a pile of white towels.

She was introduced to Gert, who looked much too old and frail to be a swimmer – at least seventy – and the substantial Mrs Malardice, fifty-something, who said 'Do call me Claire, dear. I'm the President, but we're all on first-name terms. Welcome to the Club. Are you taking the lesson?'

Iris smiled. 'I can't swim, but I'm hoping to learn, though it seems a little silly at my age.'

Josie took off her jacket. 'Never too late to learn, as I say to the adult beginners in my French class. Hang on, I'll be ready in a jiffy.' She carried on stripping off her clothes then and there, right down to the buff.

Iris was shocked rigid. She had never seen another woman without clothes on, and standing up so shamelessly! But Madam President clearly didn't think anything unusual was going on, and Gert wasn't reacting, so Iris checked the words on her lips and said nothing, though she didn't know where to put her eyes. Was it alright to look, or should you avert your gaze to – to the wallpaper? In the end, she opted for Claire Malardice's fat pink feet. Gert had buried herself in the evening paper.

Claire's chair creaked as she moved in it unwrapping a cigarette box. 'We put our handbags in lock-ups by Dick's office, in case of theft. There's all-sorts come around nowadays, and there has been the odd unexplained crime. Gert's Golden Handshake watch went missing last Christmas. Come and sit down – there's no hurry, dear, the kids don't usually come en masse for another hour or so. Smoke?' She held out the packet.

Iris sat neatly in the chair beside an old weighing machine, crossing her ankles, glad she'd painted her toenails pink last night. 'No thanks.' There was a short silence, while Claire lit up. Feeling her way, Iris asked, 'Have you been a member for long?'

Claire laughed a plump laugh. 'Long, indeed. Been a

member since I was about fifteen, m'dear. Never miss a Ladies' Day if I can help it. Woops – better get the cossie on – Dick will be waiting.' She stood up, cigarette in mouth, her eyes half-shut against the smoke, and simply dropped her towel. She shook out a faded and somewhat overstretched red swim-suit, stepped into it and swung the straps up over her shoulders. 'Hope we don't have to do lengths today. I can cope with breadths.'

'Time for the fateful weigh-in', said Josie, stepping, still stark naked, on to the scales. 'Two pounds on. Drat.' She pinched the flesh of her midriff. 'Penance – two extra lengths, and no curry this week.' She took a pristine towel from the pile. 'Claire should give that up, shouldn't she? What's the good of coming here for your health, meanwhile killing yourself off with nicotene?'

'Tis my only vice' said Claire, rolling her eyes. 'I smoke – but you eat too much, my girl. What's your sin, Iris?'

Iris smiled, tightly, but couldn't think what to say. She must have an ordinary sin, by the law of averages, but she certainly wasn't about to confess the real one, either to this company or ever.

Thankfully, Josie pulled on her costume, also red, shapeless, and dreadfully nipple-revealing. 'Ready for your lesson, Iris? Dick says he can just about fit you in. How was your day?'

'Reasonably dreadful.' Iris said, relieved at the normality of the conversation, at least. 'Can't wait till term's over.' Everyone moaned about work – actually she rather enjoyed hers, but you couldn't say so. She decided the navy lycra looked harsh against her parchment-coloured wintry skin.

'Did you manage to find a cap?' Josie dug in her bag.

'With difficulty' Iris waved the blue flower-petalled creation. 'Boots the chemist.'

'Oh, very fetching – we mostly just use these.' Josie stuffed her hair into an old grey shower-cap. 'Dick won't look at any of us now.' Her friend Josie was behaving – differently

– here. They had known each other since their schooldays, and had kept in touch while Josie brought up three children and Iris looked after her ageing parents. Josie's children had all flown the nest now and she had proved a good friend during recent months as Iris had wretchedly nursed poor Mother through her final illness. Now she, Iris, was also free and Josie had persuaded her to join the swimming club as part of the new Life Plan she'd made. 'You're young enough to start again' she'd said. 'Not yet fifty, self-sufficient unlike me, and all these school holidays to fill. You'll have a great time.'

Several other women mostly aged between about forty and sixty, had drifted into the room wafting steam from the Turkish bath. They all put on the regulation red swim-suits and shower-caps so that they looked like a school team. Iris felt self-conscious in her Marks & Sparks number and the flowery hat. Today, like all new girls, she'd have to stay quiet, watch the others, and learn the ropes. She'd soon see how people expected you to behave. Meantime she'd just have to put up with the little embarrassments. One thing was certain – she'd never, ever, be able to make herself wander around without clothes.

They went along a carpeted corridor to a room where the tiles were warm underfoot. Steam issued from a doorway labelled 'Turkish Bath'. After a brief shower, Claire led them through a cold plastic curtain to the pool.

The stretch of blue water hadn't so much as a ripple on its surface. Three trapezes were strung down one side, with a ladder leading up to the first, and there were some rings on ropes. These would be for the children, thought Iris.

Then Claire was climbing the ladder, the loose flesh on her thighs rippling slightly as she went, varicose veins bulging purple from one calf. Grabbing hold of the first trapeze and shouting 'Wheeeee' the heavy woman swung out over the pool and dropped into the water like a stone. The splash erupted over everyone.

Iris gave a little shriek, but Josie already was half-way through a long dive, entering the water like a spoon, emerging lazily and swimming back to the side, calling 'Come on in, the water's lovely.'

Carefully – she didn't want to slip now – Iris trod down the steps of the shallow end. Hot chlorine greeted her nostrils, and the warm water was waist high. Her heart was beating rather hard, for she had a deep-seated, almost superstitious fear of water. What if she fell, went under. People drowned in swimming pools – you read about it all the time. She had really just come to please Josie – she was far too old for this – it was ridiculous.

Claire was doing the crawl, racing across the pool to the far side, calling 'Dick, we're all here, come on out old boy – we've a new learner for you.'

Josie floated by on her back. 'One thing I like about this place is it's so clean. They really look after it. We start over there – come on, you'll be at the shallow end, fear not.'

Everyone was now in the pool, lining up along the side, waiting for instruction. Josie waded carefully round the edge, clinging to the rail.

'Good afternoon, ladies' a deep male voice echoed down from the office doorway. Dick appeared through a cloud of steam, a small man, perfectly proportioned and beautifully tanned, muscular as a miniature Greek hero and hairy as a faun. He wore tiny pink trunks, and a gold medallion gleamed on a chain round his neck.

The women greeted him, some teasing, some laughing, others apologising for having missed lessons.

He handed each a flat disc of polystyrene. 'Claire, you and Josie and the other experienced swimmers down to the deep end, beginners at the shallow end. We'll do widths to start with. Where's the new lady?'

Iris waved coyly, feeling again like the New Girl, not a lady at all, but young and pretty.

Josie called 'We said you'd have her swimming by

Christmas, Dick.'

He did a neat dive into the pool, making hardly a splash, and next thing he was standing in the water beside Iris. Help, she could smell his spicy aftershave through the chlorine – and she had never been so near to a man in her life, let alone a man who was half-naked. What would Mother have said? Well! She had come here for new experiences, hadn't she?

'What do I have to do?' she asked, confessing 'I'm a bit scared of water, really.'

'Nothing too drastic, Iris. We'll just try a few simple moves first, while the others are busy.'

Her back was pressed against the blue tiles of the side, as if she needed support. He showed her how to hold the polystyrene disc out in front of her, and kick her feet behind. It was rather fun, splashing along like the Jeanie Deans. Soon she was churning back and forth across the pool with the others, feeling like a paddle-steamer.

Dick shouted 'Back to the side, everyone. Put the discs away now.'

The class gathered for the next step. Everyone obediently passed their discs up the line. But the next step was more difficult.

'Widths now, faces in the water, one breath only half way across. Off you go. Now Iris.' He took her hand! And without so much as a by-your-leave he led her into deeper water! Never in her life had she held a man's hand, so strong, so warm, so full of life! 'Right, Iris, now we're going to try the legs.'

Legs?

'Legs with the arms. I'd like you to try kicking your legs just like you did with the float, and doing like this with your arms.' He mimed the arm movements, nodding at her.

Mesmerised, she copied his arm movements in the air. The next thing she knew, she was horizontal in the water, threshing her legs up and down as before, her chin cupped in Dick's hand, while his other hand supported her midriff!

She had to force herself to think about her legs and arms, trying to co-ordinate them – she'd think about the other feelings later, in the privacy of her own flat, and blush then. Now he was towing her along, his touch so light on her chin, while she kicked her legs like a two-year-old. 'Good, good' he was saying 'That's the way.' A man's hand, touching her like that. What a thrill. All of a sudden his grip slid away, his fingers just out of reach of her mouth. She kicked on, her eyes on the tips of his fingers, but her head was going under, she was sinking, and her foot touched down on the tiles.

Spluttering, rubbing the chlorine out of her eyes, she stood up. 'Sorry' she said.

He got her to try again, and again, while the others were happily splashing their way across the pool. She thought she'd never learn. For a time he left her to practice and went to work on the rest of the class. 'Claire, a dive, please today, then two lengths of breast-stroke.' What a name for a swimming movement! Crawl was bad enough. Doggy paddle was all she'd ever been capable of – and only two or three of these.

Mother would be proud of her, trying so hard to succeed, trying to overcome her fear like this, if she could see her. What really happened when people died – did their spirits live on? She'd always found it hard to believe in souls, not being religious. But if – would Mother be pleased about what she'd done – or cross? All these years of arthritis, the pain, and then the confusion so complete that she couldn't even recognise her own daughter, Iris who had given up her life to care for her. 'Accidental death,' the Coroner had said. And so it had been. Iris hadn't planned anything and it had all been like a dream – taking Mother to the bath in her shift, as usual, helping her in. Sure, it had been a little deeper than normal, but even that was only by chance. The first little push had been almost experimental, Iris had found herself wondering if Mother's hair would float out around her face like Ophelia's – and it had, it had. Only she'd had to keep pressing, pressing the head down in the water. A blessing, everyone had said. A blessing after all her suffering. Now she was in a Better Place.

At length the lesson was over and some of the ladies were leaving the pool, talking about going home to make the tea. A few young people in school uniforms wandered through, chatting, in the direction of the changing rooms.

Josie said, 'Let's stay in for a little longer – till the rush has died down in the changing-room.' Claire and Gert were cruising up and down, their shower-caps nodding as they talked. Iris decided to stay too, for a while. The pool quietened. After a time they all came together, hanging onto the side of the pool watching the ripples die down.

'How was the lesson?' Josie asked. 'You looked as if you were almost off.'

'Almost sinking, more like,' Iris said. 'D'you really think I'll ever learn?'

'Seen worse,' said Claire. 'Was worse myself when I started.'

'She was, too,' snorted Gert.

Suddenly Josie was shrieking, 'Oh look. It's another of these things.'

Claire leapt up onto the side. 'Where?'

Josie was pointing. 'There. Ugh, it's drowning – oh I can't bear to look. Dick, come here.'

Dick shouted, 'I'm on the phone.'

Iris could see a miniature storm going on, where a large brown cockroach was threshing about in the water, ruffling the calm blueness. Feeling sorry for the creature, she began to wade deeper and deeper. The water rose to her chest, to her shoulders. It was just out of reach. She went further, till the water slapped against her ear-lobes and the slant of the tiles steepened so that she knew if she took one more step she'd be out of her depth.

Reaching out, she tried paddling the water towards her with one hand to make a little current that would waft the cockroach into her other one, but it just circled on its back waving its legs in the air, whirling further away, getting exhausted now, drowning.

Claire, running round the pool, took down a long scoop from some hooks on the wall. 'If I hand you this, can you reach it, fish it out? Don't much like the creatures myself.' She wielded the ladle out across towards Iris. 'Dick, I thought we'd got rid of these beastly things.'

Grabbing the handle, Iris was able to skim the poor insect off the water, aware that she wasn't saving its life so much as ensuring it would have a quicker form of death. She waded back towards the shallow end with her catch.

Josie leapt up the steps. 'Oh, I can't bear to look – they're such dirty things. Get Dick to deal with it.' Always good at delegating, never prepared to take things into her own hands.

Quite a crowd had gathered. They clapped as Iris handed the cockroach in at the office door for Dick to destroy. This time she too would delegate the task.

She was escorted to the changing room like a hero, everyone making much of her, as though she'd done something wonderful! Of course they didn't know that she handled cockroaches every day in the school lab, not to mention stick insects and praying mantis's. What would they think of those – eating their own mates? You got quite used to nature red in tooth and claw, in the lab. 'Poor old cockroach' she said, feeling much more at home now and able to afford to be generous. 'It didn't mean you any harm.'

Everyone was stripping off wet swim-suits, throwing them into a large bin in the corner along with their towels, twists of red and white, like bent barbers' poles signifying blood and bandages, and bad luck. Iris pulled off her cap and shook out her hair. She wrapped her towel round her as though she were at the beach, peeling off her costume beneath it carefully so as not to dislodge it. The young people were getting ready for their swim. A girl passed her, naked, white, and innocent as an angel, lithe and slim – not unlike that Smith character in looks.

Women were not all the same, under their clothes, they were different. Well, they all had pubic hair and breasts and nipples and things. But there was a lot of biodegrading going on, wasn't there? Mouldering flesh. The forces of gravity were at work on older people like her, pulling at their drooping bosoms. That child's physique was really beautiful, so perfect, just like her own must have been, once, though she'd always been so worried about spots. Now she was bothered about wrinkles and the saggy bits. Perfection always seemed a mile away, for one reason or another. But she knew she looked better than Claire. And although it was awful to think that one day she might be as scraggy as Gert, at least Gert was lively enough to be quite a good swimmer. There was something comforting in that. Somehow you couldn't pretend, in your nothings, you had no uniform, no badges of office to protect you, turn you into something or somebody else. Bareness was honest.

Half-deliberately, Iris let the towel slide from her body as she went to collect her coat-hanger-ful of clothes. There were no shocked sniggers, no cat-calls. The conversations simply continued as before. No-one was noticing that, for the first time in her life, Iris McGlone was parading herself naked in public! She might as well be taking off her jacket in the staffroom at school. Come to think of it the atmosphere wasn't so different, here. She finger-dried her hair beside Josie, sharing the mirror companionably. It was a source of surprise to her that she could look herself in the eye. She wasn't a murderer, more a mercy-killer.

'Tea?' Josie smiled.

'Lovely' said Iris.

# *BURNING ROSES*

NOVEMBER IS THE TIME for burning roses. It always seems a shame to cut the stalks while the flowers still bloom, but pink petal edges are tarnished, black spot and sawfly curl and thwart the leaf-growth and winter gales rock the root-stocks loose. Have you noticed how red and white roses last longer than the rest?

Today I built a funeral pyre for all the roses in my garden. As the Gardener I have the power to flame away disease and all the mildew spores, boil thrips' eggs in their infancy and stew the unsuspecting caterpillar, to cleanse my little world. But then I came to say goodbye to you.

All the way to Greenock, bonfires smoke from farmyards, forests, gardens, parks. I pass a graveyard burning its flowers too. A low November fog fuddles the river, as though muffling the long moans of lost ships. Mournful yew trees drip last nights's rain around mossed and lichened gravestones, over the blackened building, its thin smoke-stack pointing like a gun at Heaven.

You arrive in that wooden box, piled high with roses, like a bride-doll, wrapped, a present for someone.

Two old grey crows puke and cackle on the ridge tiles. Smoke lingers, the remains of some unknown soul reluctant to leave the warm fires below for the cold unwelcoming sky.

I was there when you began to sense the chilling winds of Autumn, your mind's eye darkening with fear of the approaching storm. Yet, with what a vengeance you returned to work, taking your dogs for shorter walks, wanting to keep fit – and face the oncoming wind?

'Come to Sunday tea and let's play croquet, for a laugh' you said as Indian summer ended, 'Not Ann, she's too serious.' You never would discuss your disease, your pain, your problems. You won of course, as usual, and then we sat on the lawn round the fat and merry teapot, giggling over silly schoolday memories. 'Look,' you said at the end, trusting us, 'my hair's growing back,' and you flung the false wig up in the air. It landed on a willow branch. Your shocking egg-head gleamed bone white in that late sun, bare but for the three brief sticks of your hair along one side, all that was left of your crowning glory fallen like September grass.

A young horse went by, we talked of early days and Sam the blacksmith down the brae melting the impossible metal bars on bellowed coals, hammering scarlet toffee-iron into sparking horseshoes on his anvil. Remember, we said, how he'd sear a painless rim on live hoof so the shoe would sit true – he never hurt the horse and the wildest pony would be quiet for him. The clouds of blue burning protein wrinkled our noses.

Now the old mothers and fathers of our school-friends shuffle by, bent like old twigs, shrunken, bookit with age, not seen out-of-doors in years. Boys and girls we used to dance and fight with, swim in the buoyant brown burns, skate over thin loch ice, gather now in grey groups, mourning under the monkey-puzzle tree, whispering among themselves about you.

Behind the Garden of Rest rises a serene hill, smooth and green, and I remember you striding out over the long Autumn fields, whistling your dogs to flush the brilliant pheasant for the gun, and scare the brown grouse from cover.

You and I were wed in the same year, our hips bore fruit – how we worked to rear our children, puzzling their psychologies over steaming tea-cups. No rose without a thorn, they say, and yes, your life and mine drew blood from one another more than once, I'll say. But friends we were, and more so lately, coming from such a common past. Closer since the day they pruned a breast to stop your rot, and I first heard the cough that gagged your laughter, learned of the searing rays, the chemicals with which they tried to cleanse and singe your shrinking body.

Today the smells of Autumn's spent fruitfulness weave like evil spells round the sombre queue at your last doorway. They say the young always have a big crowd – today there's standing-room only for most of us. And you lie there, rotting already, hygienically hidden beneath your flowers, while two hundred of us sing bright hymns of praise – your favourites – gifts to your God, seeming to chant to heaven, till thinking of you stops the song in my throat and tears wash out the sound.

Now all is hushed. At last they drew the dark veil over all the blossoms and the pretty little cards, and you.

Old machinery creaks through the obsequious prayers as you are processed through yet another system, automatically. You enter your furnace, alone.

Your old mother is left to run the gauntlet of two hundred hands, while all the friends of our early life walk out into the dim November sun, deprived of you, yet with a certain feeling of relief quickening their steps.

The chimney stack exhales, its breath reeking of burnt bone, like old Sam's smithy, the smoke blowing down, blurring folk into wraiths floating through the evergreens towards the car-park. Could that be you, already, dimming down the sunbeam, darkening the dead stones, choking our lungs? Are you not angry, a furious spirit cheated of at least a score of your allotted years?

Home after your wake, the tears dried on my cheeks, at dusk I stir the ashes of my flowers. The bonfire is dead – it seems a shame I had to burn my roses.

# A HOT FLUSH IN WINTER

IT'S HARD for a woman to rise above the physical. We have the bloody inconvenience and discomfort of menstruation, the messier side of sex, followed by fecundity, childbirth and breast-feeding. Statistics show that 90% of us become 'difficult' before each period because of pre-menstrual syndrome (P.M.S.) for thirty to forty years of our working lives, till the menopause comes along to mellow our moods. And we've only just begun to spend our tampon money on higher things when we're zapped with hot flushes.

Hot flushes are an unsexy fact of life. The British Medical Association describes them coolly as a 'reddening of the face, neck, and upper trunk usually caused by decreased oestrogen hormone production'. No real problem, it seems.

In fact it's a very public happening. A Catherine-wheel of sparks starts spinning in the solar plexus, whirling in ever-widening circles till one's whole body burns in a thought-defeating blush. The unfortunate turn scarlet, most of us go all varnished-looking and, for the worst-affected, pailfuls of sweat rain from every pore, running down our necks, soaking through our shirts, and making us hyperventilate as though we've just come in from a ten-mile run.

It feels claustrophobic in there among our clothes, especially when we're bundled up in winter woollies. There's a desperate desire to rip everything off and stand naked in some cooling breeze, issuing steam like a threatening volcano. If you see a woman at a business lunch tearing off scarves and ripping open the buttons of her cleavage she's not trying to clinch a deal with her body, she's simply chasing another flush. Battery-operated fans help some of my contemporaries, others cool off with a handbag-sized water spray. Myself, I prefer a good strong Scottish gale, the colder the better and preferably dished up with hailstones.

Hill-walking to discourage the decalcification of middle-aged female bones, I stomp along into a freezing head-wind wearing only a sleeveless summer top and shorts. Passing through blizzards I look behind me, to see a stream of crystal drops, a kind of one-woman-wide rainstorm, in my wake as my body-heat melts the flying ice.

During a weekly swimming lesson, endured to keep the ageing ticker tocking, I risk a dive. Between air and water a flush strikes and I enter the pool with a sizzle like a soldering iron, a red-hot poker quenching itself in champagne. Steam-filled bubbles boil to the surface and I emerge scarlet and seething with heat like a well-fried pudding supper.

Driving home, I evaporate in another flush so that not only the windscreen, but also the side-windows and the mirror, fog up dangerously. The last thing I want is to turn up the heater – so all the windows are opened causing howls of anguish from frozen passengers.

A regular feature of my night-life these days includes flinging the duvet from my naked body while the winter wind shrieks through the unheated bedroom. One night in January we woke up under a blanket of snow. My consort suffers regularly from hypothermia, and occasionally frost-bitten toes clatter to the ground.

Hormone Replacement Therapy (H.R.T.) is, theoretic-ally, the cure. In America there are seventy year-olds still on

H.R.T. Can you imagine putting up with periods and, presumably, P.M.S. till you're seventy? Because that, it seems, is the fee.

No matter what sort of work we're involved in, our hormones interfere. Mood swings are the worst, because they affect judgement, exam performance, but hot flushes affect concentration. Just as you're about to deliver the denouement to a rousing political speech, the punchline to your sales pitch, the last masterstroke to your work of art – bang! The fireworks are bursting inside you again.

# THE
# SEVENTH
# WAVE

VERA'S FIFTY YEAR-OLD LUNGS strained for breath and her heart was pounding as she reached the top tread of the metal stairway. A flush of sweat bloomed over her body. Shrieks echoed up through the steamy warmth from the children swimming below. The young attendant dragged a wet mat from the pile by the flumes and drooped it over his arm. He looked bored to death. Cold drips fell on her from the roof.

She looked at the torn ticket in her hand, bestowed on her so generously, so trustingly, by her grand-daughter Jeannie who was at this minute awaiting her arrival down there in the pool.

She'd never have the guts to do it. She was afraid of taking the plunge into that plastic tube. It would give you the kind of spinning-away feeling you got just as you were going under anaesthetics, or in the nightmare where you were falling, falling, down some dark and bottomless well. She'd always hated that particular dream. She was afraid of closed-in spaces, and of heights. There were quite a lot of things she was afraid of, really.

The mouths of the twin flumes opened, cavernous and terrifying, in front of her, one pink, one blue, like the diagrams of arteries and veins she'd had to draw at school years ago. All very well for the kids, but could she ever find the courage to launch herself into these unknown convolutions? She strongly doubted it. Yet she'd feel such a fool if she had to climb ignominiously down the stairs she'd so recently managed to get herself up. She wished now she hadn't bothered.

Out beyond the steam-streaked windows you could see the February landscape, chilled into grey immobility under its shroud of frozen slush. The beach merged greyly into the pale grey sea which folded and crumpled itself into a blurred horizon of dull grey clouds.

'I think you should come in tomorrow,' the surgeon had said in the morning. 'Take the rest of today to think it over, it's your decision. Let the hospital know before five. It's always better not to delay with these things.'

Brooding at home alone had been hopeless, so Vera had phoned her daughter Flo, offered to bring this grandchild to the sports centre after school as she sometimes did on Wednesdays. But today was Thursday and Flo had been a little surprised.

Vera had muttered something about wanting a little company to take her mind off a problem. Flo hadn't enquired what it was, glad to have the child usefully amused while she finished off some work.

'Och Granny, have you no' gone yet?' Wee Jeannie's disgusted face appeared round the bend in the stairway, followed by the dripping ten-year-old torso in its scarlet swimsuit, and the long lanky legs with the knobbly knees that were so like Flo's. 'Come on Granny, it's easy. You just fling your bum over the edge and you're away!'

'Bottom, love,' Vera corrected automatically. 'Maybe I'll manage it in a minute. To tell you the truth I'm a bit scared. You go on Jeannie, have your turn.'

'Did you see me scooshing out the end Granny?' Jeannie held up her wrist for the attendant to tear off another section of the pricey strip-ticket you'd to buy them for the flumes. 'I waved at you. That's me been five times. I'm on my belly this time – look. You come after me, right?' For an instant the commanding green eyes held Vera's, then with a yelp of glee Jeannie flung herself into the stream of rushing water, waggling delighted toes as she swooshed round the first bend and out of sight.

Vera said 'Tummy dear, not belly' to the splash-filled air.

She glanced at the young attendant. He must think her a right poultice. He probably thought she was far too old to be up here anyway. But no, he appeared to be staring into vacant space, his mind switched off. True enough, it must be pretty boring just standing there tearing tickets off and handling wet mats all day. He'd not care one way or the other whether she dared to take the plunge or no.

Outside snaked the two flumes, the pink and the blue, contorting like the agonised intestines of some dis-embowelled beast before spiralling back into the body of the building to disgorge their contents into the swirling cauldron beneath her feet.

'Quite a major operation,' the surgeon had said. 'We won't know the whole story till we've opened you up.'

If only you could be certain you'd be all right in the end. If only you knew you'd be able to stand the pain. Vera remembered childbirth. She'd coped – well, you had to. With childbirth you didn't have a choice. But she hadn't coped all that well, she didn't feel particularly proud of not coping. Everyone else seemed to. But she'd screamed a lot when you weren't suppposed to.

If only she was a child again herself, when mother knew best, and would always tell you what to do, and cuddle you and make you better. But mother had been dead many a long year. There was no-one left to make decisions for Vera. And this time the alternatives were so appalling.

'Gran – ny!' A shriek louder than the rest wafted up. Jeannie was waving frantically from the pool. 'Did you see me?'

Vera waved back. The child was such a delight to her.

These grandchildren were all pleasure, not like her own children had been, what with all the anxieties, the fears for their morals, their health, their futures.

Last time she'd been taken to hospital, bleeding like a butcher's shop, she'd lost her fruitful womb. Better off without it, they'd said. They'd been right too, though she'd never quite got over the feeling of being neutered, like the cat. But that hadn't been a matter of life and death, and she'd been younger then. Even so, the weakness afterwards had wearied her for months.

'Exercise,' they'd said in Physiotherapy after a while. 'Go swimming.' So she'd started coming here to the centre and she'd learned how to swim. Right enough, you never were too old to learn. Now she enjoyed bringing the little ones, watching them come on. Flo trusted her with them because she was so good in the water.

Vera was quite proud of being able to say to her contemporaries in an airy way 'I'm away to the baths with the children today – my daughter's busy at work so I'm taking them for their swimming lesson.'

A queue of youths had formed on the stair. They were joking and laughing, jostling each other, kidding on they were men. Unemployed, that they were free to come swimming at this time of day, Vera thought. What a waste of their healthy young lives.

She heard Jeannie's voice behind them chattering away. She would go with Jeannie. She must find the courage, to please the child.

One by one the lithe young bodies leapt into the fearsome pink flume, revelling in the sheer physical action, every muscle working to achieve maximum speed.

Vera gripped the chrome balustrade, looking down into the dappled turquoise of the pool beneath, her head already spinning slightly. She felt the rising wobble of panic – she'd never been a one for helter-skelters or even merry-go-rounds. For a moment she allowed the giddiness to sweep over her.

But no, she would not let it overcome her. Feel the sensation, she told herself, feel it and then try to deal with it.

'Were you watching Granny?' Jeannie's perky features bounced towards her. 'Did I come out fast?'

'Like a cork out of a bottle,' Vera smiled.

'See Granny, you'd like it fine. It's great. Right, this time I'll go in the big tube, that one,' she pointed to the pink flume. 'I've no' done it yet 'cos I'm feart. You go in the blue one. We'll start at the same time. Then we'll both be feart the same, OK?'

'But won't it be too fast for you? And what if the blue one's too fast for me?'

'Och Granny! If you sit yoursel' up you slow down. Then, if you want to go a wee bit faster, you lie back. Look.' Jeannie prostrated herself and demonstrated the positions. 'Come on Granny, you do it.' The green eyes demanded Vera's obedience.

Casting a self-conscious glance at the attendant, Vera did as she was told.

Jeannie jumped up. 'See? You can do it fine. Come on we'll go together.'

Vera's stomach lurched within her as she got up. Feel the fear, she told herself, then deal with it. But don't let it beat you.

Jeannie took her by the hand. The attendant placed the mat on the flume's lip for her. She watched not the rushing water, not the blue tunnel in front of her, but only the child.

The green eyes held hers as Jeannie plonked herself at the throat of the pink tube. The child's voice was drowned by the gargling water, but the sleek head nodded as the little hands showed Vera how to hold the sides of the mat up. The eyes began to twinkle with excitement as the wee pink mouth mimed 'One, two, three, go!'

Holding her breath, copying every movement of the child's, Vera tipped herself over the edge into the blue abyss.

For a moment she was washed downwards on her back,

helpless, round the first bend gathering speed, her brain swirling, numb. Gradually she came to, to see the translucent blueness of everything, to hear the silence, feel the purity of clear water that took her with such soft strength. 'Sit up' the child's voice came back to her 'If you want to slow down.' She tried, and it worked. She could control how fast she went. She sped round a wide spiral. This is me going down the drain, she thought surprising herself with a giggle, then lurching into a sudden incline. You couldn't take the wrong turning here, the tube took care of that.

She lay back to keep moving over a flatter section, feeling more confident of being in control of her speed. But as she did so the mat slipped from under her. She tried sitting up, but as she cruised over each joining ridge the bump shuddered her spine painfully. She decided to slide on recumbent, relaxed, going with the stream. Moving faster now out of choice, she began to enjoy herself. Wheeee, this was great, like being a child again, like being birled round by your Daddy.

Abruptly she fell over a harder joint. Then she was sinking, sinking so deeply into a fizz of foam, deep into the soft warmness.

Caught by surprise, she hadn't much air in her lungs. Now she needed to drag in a breath more than anything in the world. She'd never get to the surface in time, and anyway, where was it? Panic opened her eyes. Through the chlorine-laden blurr she saw a little kicking foot just above her, a streak of scarlet swimsuit. Thrusting wildly she followed it upwards.

With a burst of joy and relief she surfaced, spluttering, sucking in great gusts of air.

'Hey Granny!' the child popped out of the water, effervescing, spraying droplets, 'You done it!' She grinned through her hair 'Isn't it no' great, Granny?'

This child was her lucky mascot. For her Vera would do anything, now.

They hugged each other then swam towards the side of the catchment tank. Vera looked up at the platform from which she'd slid. What a long way she'd fallen. To her surprise the young attendant was waving at them. She raised an arm. Not scared now, not drowning, she thought, but triumphant. She'd felt the fear, but she'd been the boss, she hadn't let the fear rule her. She'd ridden the flume and survived. Maybe this was how you felt when you'd done your first free-fall like these parachutists on the telly.

Perhaps there were more things you could do in this life, new things you could try.

Her fear of hospitals was the next one she'd be tackling. Six times she'd been taken to hospital against her will. Her dear husband had died in one. No wonder she was scared. Well you couldn't feel in charge of your own body once the nurses got at you, and it was all so public. You might snore in the ward, or not be able to be brave enough, you might be sick or wet the bed.

But maybe the risk was worth taking. It would be worth putting up with a bit of discomfort if it meant you'd stay alive a while longer and be able to watch your little ones grow up. If you allowed the fear to rule you, if you refused to go for the operation, what then?

She dragged her body up the chrome steps. She was amazed how heavy she felt after the buoyancy of the water.

Jeannie sparkled above her 'I done it! The pink tube was real speedy, Gran. Come on – I've still two tickets left.' Generously she held out a piece of the precious strip to Vera.

'Thanks hen, but once is enough for me today. You use them now, while I go and wash my hair in the showers. It'll need to be clean for the hospital tonight. But maybe I'll get to ride the flumes with you again one day, when I'm better.' Vera gave the child a little push. 'On you go now. See and try the pink one again, it's more exciting when it's scary.'

# PEGGY'S WALK

PEGGY SHUT the security door of the close firmly behind her. They weans fae up the stair were aye leavin' it open. She sniffed the Govan air. No a bad evenin' for October. Yon Ian McAskill had put double raindrops and a black cloud over Glasgow for tonight – but by the time the storm came she'd be safely home again, wi' her paper, a smoke, good hot tea in her bone china cup wi' the blue roses round it, and the antics of *Take The High Road* to keep her mind off the cold.

Peggy stepped out along the pavement, head high, aware that her long legs looked fine in their brown boots, the blue chiffon scarf matched her eyes, and the tan coat showed off her hair that was still as red as the day she'd clicked wi' big Danny Elliott. Her pals used to say she carried her years weel. They must o' been richt enough, because here wis she at seventy-five and no wan o' them left. Now there was only the kirk social wance a week. But she'd no' complain. She'd no run greetin' tae Angela. She, Peggy Elliott, could luik efter herself.

Life had been guid tae her. She fingered the purse in her pocket. She'd worked hard a' her days, the biscuit factory in winter, all sorts of jobs in the summers when she'd been

young, when Angela came along she'd done caretakin' so she
could stay at hame. Even now she'd aye a wee bit put by even
if yon pension was a joke and they kep sendin' they forms
you couldnae understaun. She'd never borrowed a penny in
her life, and she owed nothin' tae naebody.

The only two wishes she had in her heart were that Danny
was still here to enjoy life wi' her and that Angela didnae live
so far away.

The corner shop was quiet – all the wee families home at
their teas. There was only an old man, smelling of piss, buying
crisps and a can of Irn Bru. Peggy picked up the *Evening Times*
– it was heavy being Friday – and checked the date: 10th
October 1991 – she'd picked up papers twa days auld and
mair before, ye had tae be switched on. Her hand picked up
a packet of Consulate, appreciating the slippery cellophane.
Soon there would be the pleasure of stripping it off, the
crackle to be followed by the fresh tobacco smell.

She exchanged a word with Mr Hassan. Nae harm to the
darkies – they had to work for their living just like everyone
else. Naebody in their right minds wid keep a shop round
here, what wi' the vandals, the break-ins and the grafitti.
Hassan's shop wis like Fort Knox wi' its battered bolts and
bars, and wire mesh ower the windaes. His wife did days, and
he worked through the night. Likely he couldnae close for
fear of the vandals. He'd get business frae the Hospital folk,
the only shift workers left in Govan since the yards closed.

Peggy decided on a wee dauner in the park. It would pit
aff the moment of smoking, prove she still had some
self-control even if she couldnae always get her insides to do
what she wanted. Her waterworks would be a'right tonight
though – she'd been to the toilet just before she came out.
Oh she'd show her body who was boss. She folded the
newspaper into her shoulder bag.

She crossed the road at the green man. Her eyes were
guid enough thank God, but you'd tae be careful, wi' the rush
hour on.

The last of the day wis dyin' away, street lights warming from pink till they turned the green palings and the grass blackie- orange. The park gates were still open. Big heaps of leaves lay under each tree. They looked awful nice. She'd scuffle her feet through them for the rustly feel. There was naebody about to lauch at her except an auld man in a bunnet, and you didnae need tae pay ony heed tae him, sittin' there on the bench swiggin' his carry-oot.

Crunch crunch went the leaves, like crisps. She was a daft auld buddie – second childhood right enough – dotage more likely. What wid Angela in her posh bought hoose say if she could see her mither noo? Peggy giggled.

She'd used tae play in the leaves wi' the weans, when she'd had thon wee job up at the Botanics. They'd had her runnin' aboot like a wean hersel', and a' the parkies blawin' their whistles to get them aff the grass. Huh, the grass wis where the weans should be, no skinnin' their knees on the tarmac, in all the dog's dirt.

That had been guid work. She'd taken it on impulse – Mother's Help – the day her Angela had left home. Angela had said she preferred to live in a flat like the other Art students, and Peggy hadn't known how to bear the loss of her only child. So she'd put all her energy into raising these other weans, takin' them tae nursery, fetchin' them and gettin' their tea, while their mither was out working. Later when she'd had tae meet them at the Primary school gates and take them home fur their tea, it had been almost like the auld times wi' Angela. Weans wis the same the warld ower.

Maw hud been right – she aye said you never knew whit wis roon the next corner, guid or bad.

The year when Danny had died so suddenly, the woman had a late baby and asked Peggy to stay on. She'd stayed on till that wean went tae school and it wis time tae start drawin' her pension.

The gates at the far end of the park were closed and padlocked. Peggy stood for a few minutes, watching the lines of brightly lit buses full of workers going home. Each one stopped at the corner to let folk off, groups of chattering girls, weary-looking men. It made her feel lonely. She wished somebody was coming home to her.

She turned her back on the lights and wandered down the side path, the traffic streaming by down the main road. Funny there werenae any caurs the nicht. She missed the rattlin' and clangin', the blue sparks aff the wires. Maybe there wis a strike on. She could fair go a ride on a caur noo. When she'd been a wee lass, Maw wid take her on the caurs, for a treat.

Here, it was time she went to visit Maw. She'd go now – it wasnae far. She should go more often, but the auld wumman was that carnapcious these days, unless she'd had a win at the Bingo. Ann, the youngest, could handle her better.

Peggy set off along the main road. She'd aye known where her duty lay.

Govan had changed. Streets were funny that way. It wasnae the road itself you knew, but the buildin's. Her Danny had been workin' on some o' they sites when they first met, helpin' tae modernise Glasgow, as he wid say. Hauf o' his buildin's had got smashed by the bombs in the war. That wis while they were courting. After the war they were merrit. They'd go walking on a Sunday, make up wee stories aboot the folk that lived in the tenement flats they passed.

One day Danny had died in their street. He was walkin' hame with the mornin' paper for her. Everyone said it was a blessing, he never had tae go to the hospital. But it wasnae a blessin' tae her. She loved Danny and she wanted him wi' her for ever. He'd been a guid man, worked hard for her and Angela. Right up tae that last mornin' he wid aye gie her a wee kiss afore he left her, and oh they'd had some good laughs together over the years. He'd been like the best o' friens and a lover rolled intae wan.

She came to a side road. There were fewer lights here and

it lay dark and deserted between its tenements. Annie's street.
Modernisation hadnae struck here, that wis for sure. She
stepped into the close. It smelt of earth, gas and urine.
Imagine livin' in a hoose wi nae lavvy these days. Annie had
tae go doon the back-court every time she needed.

Peggy chapped the door on the left. Inside were voices
raised in argument. That wasnae like Ann's faimily. She
rapped louder. Whit wis goin' on?

Shuffling footsteps. The door opens and an auld geyser
sticks his face oot 'Whit dae ye want?'

'Ann?' Even as the word came, Peggy's memory faltered.
'There nae Ann here hen.' The man shut the door.

She turned away uncertainly. She felt daft, and afraid.
Annie was dead, and somehow she'd forgotten. This wisnae
Annie's street at all. And if it wisnae, then where wis she?
Walking out along the street with bits and pieces of memory
drifting in and out of her mind like leaves on the wind, she
remembered Annie's funeral.

They'd agreed on no black. Annie couldnae abide
blackness. She'd aye loved pretty things, flowers, china, lace.
But she couldnae mak life pretty. Annie's man had died at
thirty leavin' her tae work and rear their weans. When she'd
retired – allow Annie – she'd went tae town. Everythin' in
the hoose – rosy pink. Peggy smiled. Annie's kids had made
a lovely funeral for their mum, and all the flowers, the
tablecloths, the napkins, even the wee fancy cakes –
everything – had been pink.

The street met the river with a barricade of rusty palings.
Peggy stopped for a look. Oh what she'd do for a smoke. She
felt in her bag and found her fags nestling against Danny's
old lighter. Just one, then she'd get on her way. A cold wind
came lifting off the Clyde, smelling of dark things and dirty
water. She'd not stop long.

She split the silky cellophane in a series of automatic
movements – the lifting out of the cigarette, the tapping three
times on the packet to settle the tobacco, the screwing up of

her eyes against the flame as she lit up and that first beautiful drag. She inhaled deeply.

The river rolled silently past her feet, streaked with orange and black. There should be a ferry to take you across. Maybe it wasnae time for it yet.

The water minded her o' the Canal, and the Fairy Queen. Oh whit a job that wis, and her and her pal Josie just lasses o' seventeen. The laughs they'd had. Waitresses on the canal boat for a whole summer. Sometimes they'd jump ship on the way to Edinburgh, when the servin' wis over. The dancin' at Bo'ness wis great. They'd slip back ontae the boat again on its wey back tae Glasgow. Oh and the boss wid gie them laldy if he caught them at it.

A man, staggering slightly from drink, had come down the far side of the street. He was peeing into the river. ''R y'awright hen? Dis yer mither knaw ye'r oot?' He sniggered mushily. Who did he think he wis? Disgustin'.

Peggy put her nose in the air and stalked off. You were best tae no argue wi' them when they were fu'.

At the top of the street she didn't know whether to turn left or right. She fought for some memory of where she was going, some reason to choose a direction. She felt in her bag for clues. The *Times*. Aye, she'd been to get the *Times* fur Maw. She couldnae be faur frae Maw's close noo.

She was tiring. There was nothing but boarded-up shops here. Och she was daft. She must have taken a wrong turnin' somewhere. She'd have to ask the way. To her ain mither's hoose! But there was naebody about tae ask.

The wind gasped through the close mouths, skirling leaves and chip-papers round her feet. She shivered suddenly. Need to get a move on, it was getting colder. And she was beginning to need the lavvy. Uncertainly, she squinted to see the name of the next street. Someone had broken half the sign off and left only 'frew Road. Angela used to say 'frew' instead of 'through', when she was a wee lassie. Who was this Angela she kept thinking about – must be a wee sister. For the life of her she couldnae mind. Fancy that, you couldnae mind your ain sisters! Traffic roared somewhere ahead. Good, there'd be some life about, someone she could ask the way. She began to walk more quickly.

The concrete island was brightly lit, cars swooshing round like it wis a carousel at the shows, beamin' their lights intae her eyes. The shows – Glasgow Green at the Fair – no, she must keep her mind on whit she wis daein' here. Wan false move and it wid be curtains for Peggy Elliott. Look left, look right, listen. No green man here to help you cross. A gap in the traffic. Now.

She'd all but reached the other side when another set of headlights blinded her. She did a wee jump towards the kerb, but her legs were tired and wouldn't obey her. She crunched over on her left ankle and went her length. For several minutes she lay there, fists knuckling the pavement in agony, screwing up her face so's not to let the pain scream out.

When the first wrenching soreness had eased a bit she spoke sternly to herself. 'Get up wumman. Ye canna sit here a' nicht. There naebody comin' tae carry ye hame.'

Her bag had hit the fence and emptied itself. She crawled over and scrabbled together what she could see. In a minute she'd get up. Her right hand was sore where she'd landed on it. The pain in her ankle had dulled to a hot throbbing. She heaved herself up and tested her weight on it. As the cold wind blew through her clothes she realised she'd wet herself a wee bit.

Holding onto the fence that ran alongside the pavement, Peggy hobbled on.

Whit else could she dae? Here she wis, no idea which road she wis on nor even whaur she was gaun. Whit wis she daen oot here in the middle o' the night? She tried to force her mind to remember, to push back the fog that seemed to enclose it and find some sense of order to keep down the rising panic. Had she been at work? Oot tae the flicks? Maybe oot for her tea tae some new frien's hoose, aye that wid be it likely. That wid explain how she was lost, how she didnae know the street she wis on. Stupit auld bachle that she wis. A wry smile came to her lips – well at least she could lauch at herself.

Carefully she counted over her options. She couldnae wait a' nicht for the buses to start up again. She felt in her bag for her bus pass. Aye, it wis there, and her fags and lighter – but where was her purse? She stopped under a streetlight, peering into her bag. Her purse had gone.

No bus fare.

Peggy hirpled on. Her ankle hurt and oh she wis that weary. The road seemed to stretch for ever. For a minute she considered trying to thumb a lift. But where to? And Peggy Elliott hud never asked for charity. Anyway, it wisnae wise, takin' lifts.

She'd need to find a bus shelter. She could squat down behind it to relieve herself. Later, when the workers buses started she'd talk her way on – kid on she wis just a stupit auld wumman.

There must be a shelter soon.

She wid count the street lights. Why hud they put them sae faur apart on this road? The Cooncil grudgin' money as usual. Her bladder would burst soon.

A gateway opened beside her. She hesitated. A brass plaque told her it was a dentist's house. She hadn't needed a dentist since she'd had her full set made at the dental hospital.

She went a little way up the drive. Dimly a light showed through a side window. She chapped the door. She'd ask very politely if she could use their toilet. Then she'd ask to use the phone. A dentist would have a telephone.

Peggy drew herself up to her full height. They wouldnae let you in if they didnae think you looked respectable. She knocked again.

Nothing happened.

Of course – she hadnae seen the doorbell. Likely the family wid be watching the telly and wouldnae have heard her knock. She pressed the little white button in its brass square. Far away she could hear the bell ringing.

Nobody came.

Peggy stepped carefully off the porch and limped round towards where the light glimmered from a side window. It was pitch- dark up here away from the street lights. The window had frosted glass so you couldnae see in. Maybe it wis a bathroom, and whoever lived there wis havin' a shower. That wid be why they hadnae come tae the door. She'd all but reached the window when her shins cracked against a low brick wall and she pitched forward into jaggy bushes.

Thorns scraped her face and hands as she went down. Urine flooded warmly through her skirt like blood. Peggy wept.

She huddled there for a long time, the need for hurry gone. Rain began to fall, blown sidyways by the wind, but it was the shivering that brought her to her senses, the squalls of deeper shuddering. She wid have tae get hersel' out o' here somehow, before she got hypothermia, before they found her.

Dragging her sleeves and her coat from the thorns bit by bit, grimacing as the prickles reluctantly gave her up, she tore free of the bush. She couldnae find her woolly hat, and her hair straggled down over her face. Her good tights were laddered and blood seeped through at the knees.

Somehow she got herself back over the wall. Dragging one foot after the other, thighs chafing with wetness, Peggy got herself to the roadway.

The moon had come out from behind rags of cloud, all squinty-looking. The wind carried a familiar smell – smoke fae a coal fire. Under the next streetlight sat a wee orange hut. A brazier burned brightly in its entrance.

Peggy half crawled towards it. Oh whit she'd dae for a wee bit heat.

A watchman sat inside, drinking from a steaming can. At that moment he wouldn't have been a more welcome sight if he'd been a king in a fairy castle.

Now he'd seen her. "R y'awright hen?'

'Aye, maybe A am.'

'Have ye hud a wee drink, eh?'

Peggy stood up and almost fell as she took a final step towards the brazier. A retort came to her lips and stopped there. She shook her head, tears coursing down her cheeks.

'Did ye miss the bus then?'

From somewhere she summoned up some spirit. 'Is yon a sup o' tea you're haein'?' She had never begged in her life. She'd think o' how tae repay the man later.

'Ye're as weel comin' in oot the cauld, missus.' The old man upturned a pail and offered it to her as though it was a throne.

The need for warmth was too much for her. Knowing she smelled of stale urine she kept her legs as close together as she could, squeezing past the brazier and into the shelter.

She sat gingerly on the bucket, not sure if it would hold her. 'A feel like oor Wullie' she said, smiling uncertainly up at him.

He passed his can to her. The tea was hot and tarry. Well drawn, the way she liked it, with milk and plenty o' sugar. Steam fogged her eyes as she inhaled the warmth before starting to sup delicately at the side of the can he hadnae touched. The metal edge wis that hot, and you got the tinny taste and the coal-soot in wi' the tea. But it was pure nectar. After a few minutes she set down the can and opened her shoulder-bag, being careful not to let him see in – she wasnae daft. 'Could ye use a smoke?' She lifted out the packet of Consulate. It took her cold fingers a moment to open the lid.

Feeling good that she'd been able to offer something, she found herself thankful the man wasnae a talker. They sat side by side smoking in silence. Peggy stared into the fire. They said Hell wis like that, a burnin' furnace where ye had tae roast for ever, if ye'd been bad. She didnae know how bad you'd had tae be. She'd aye liked seein' pictures in the red hot

coals. She let her eyes roam down into the brazier, past the
flames dancin' on top all purple and blue and green like wee
chiffon scarves flappin' frae a clothes line, down through the
red and gold caverns, in among the scarlet tunnels. She didn't
see the man lift his phone, didn't hear him speak softly into
it.

A white car drew up by the kerb. Its whirling blue light
stopped and a policeman got out.

He poked his head into the hut. 'Is that the auld wino?'

The hospital had fluorescent lights and rows of plastic
seats. The policeman handed Peggy a mug of tea. The mug
was made of white earthenware, like a chantie, and felt thick
and coarse against her mouth.

After they'd bathed her she lay between stiff white sheets
that rustled over the waterproof mattress. There were sides
like on a cot. Second childhood right enough. Young people
in white coats stood at the end of her bed talking. One word
kept popping out at her – 'dementia'. 'First episode of
dementia,' they said. Reminded her o' the name o' a lassie
she'd been at the school wi' – Clementia or somethin'. Why
did they have to keep usin' they foreign words when there
wis guid Scots yins in their heids?

This wee nurse kept wakin' her up wi' stupit questions –
'What day is it?' 'A don't know.' 'What time is it?' 'Openin'
time.' 'What town is this?' 'You think A'm daft, don't ye?'
'What's your name?' 'Peggy. Mrs Elliott to you. When ma
man Danny comes fur me he'll tell yez. Noo, gie us peace
hen.' Peggy rolled over onto her side enjoying the sweet clean
pillow, and curled her sore legs up, crossing her feet comfily.
So – they thought she had the DTs. She'd show them, when
she signed herself out in the morning. Peggy slept.

# *SWAN SONG PASSING*

ANNA SAT IN THE BOW of the little white motorboat, the sole passenger. Its noise disturbed the tranquility of the Lake of Menteith, over which the pale October sun cast a gentle light. The island, Inchmahome, lay half-hidden, wreathed around with mist, and wood-smoke from some bonfire perfumed the air.

'I'll be a while coming back,' said the boatman. 'I'm on myself, and I've my dinner to get. Bob McCurtain the groundsman is away his holidays, now the season's over here.' The boat nudged in to the jetty and he stepped out to tie up. 'I'll maybe be about an hour and a half – will you be all right?'

'Fine, thanks.' Anna walked up the jetty.

'Are you wanting a guidebook or postcards from the hut, before I go?'

'Good idea. I might as well read something while I'm here. Yes, please.' It would be a kind of revision course on all that Dave had told her about the place.

The hut smelt of creosote. The boatman rustled about

and produced some leaflets. 'There's one about Queen Mary too. Did you know she stayed here once?' He handed her a thin pamphlet with the sombre portrait of Mary Queen of Scots on its cover. 'It's £1. Now mind, you'll be on your own quite a while.'

Anna smiled bitterly to herself. On her own she certainly was. 'I shall be quite happy, thanks.'

She stood by the jetty as the boat circled away, wrinkling a twist of wake on the shiny water. While the engine puttered into silence and the water settled to mirror-stillness again, Anna stayed where she was, trying to sense the mood of the island today, remembering its atmosphere of quiet attentiveness, expectancy. Perhaps in this place of peace she would find new direction, be able to rediscover her decisiveness, force her frozen mind to take on the responsibility for telling her what to do with her life, make things matter again.

Silence embalmed the place. No breath of air stirred. Autumn was well-advanced, warm fumes of fungus, mosses and trodden leaves rising from the damp earth like the ghosts of past summers. Most of the trees were already bare, skeleton-shapes blown clean by last week's gales, though the plane-tree beside the ruined Priory was holding on to the last of its leaves. She looked at the guide book. Could that tree truly have been planted by the doomed Queen of Scots all those centuries ago – or was it a myth for tourists such as herself? The long dark eyes of the medieval queen on the cover of the guide book seemed to gaze directly into hers, neither smiling nor sorrowful, revealing nothing. Inside was the information that Mary had only visited this place briefly as a child. What had this island been like then? And the young life of a little sixteenth century French-Scottish aristocrat – had that been happy, or sad? Anna's knowledge of Scottish history amounted to a few half-remembered shreds, mostly about battles and beheadings, from her own schooldays. What a luxury it was for her to have time to indulge, for once, in such pointless wonderings.

A gaunt grey tower thrust its fractured edges upwards into dark veils of cypress, sightless windows half-hidden by branches. Anna jumped as a crow scuffled on a gargoyle's snout, squawking derisively at her as it flew away across the lake like a departing devil. She shivered a little, drifting into the ruined nave, where a single sunbeam filtering through the shadows pointed out the blank eroded eyes and features of strange little faces carved in the stone-work. They watched her quietly, as though waiting. The sunbeam splashed on to a worn tombstone at her feet, picking out naively carved skulls and cross-bones. A frisson prickled her backbone.

Common sense told her not to allow irrational fears to take over – this had been a holy place, so any ghosts would be friendly enough – not that she believed in such things.

A blur of white crossed her vision, floating down to land across her sleeve. It was a long feather. She turned it over, examining its immaculate strength, its downy softness where quill had met skin. Funny to think people used to write with such instruments. Sometimes, as a child, she'd tried to make quill-pens, dipping them in ink which they always spattered across the page in blots and streaks. Her friends had thought she was crazy, not that she'd ever had many. She had always been a loner, preferring the company of books to that of people. The only child of old parents, both dead now, she had found her contemporaries immature, silly. Now she was thirty-five and her contemporaries were busy bringing up the next generation, their lives channelled into a different purpose to hers, till now. She sighed again, sticking the long feather in her buttonhole. It was such a relief to be completely alone at last, to be free finally to cry without distorting her public face, without distressing others. But only one or two tears fell as she walked on through the ruins.

Last time she'd been here was early summer, oh, all of seven years ago. It had been such a hot day! She and Dave had wandered along the Nun's Walk under a canopy of tender new leaves, washed in their green light, exulting in the lush perfumes from the sea of bluebells at their feet, so entwined in the closeness of their love. He had told her the legend of the little nun, drowned in a cruel trick to stop her meeting her lover, a young monk from the Priory. He had told her of his ancestors who had been gardeners on the island since beyond the beginnings of history, and he had told her of the little Queen of Scots.

That year had seen her own flowering. She had been sent on a prizewinning trip to New York, as part of her brilliant career, where she had met Dave and fallen so in love with him that her work had shrunk into insignificance. They had married in a dream of sunlight, white lace and roses, had spent their honeymoon near this lake, before moving back to London where she had discovered almost immediately that she was pregnant. Their summer had passed too soon.

For the first time, sobs welled up from the bottom of her heart, spilling over the dam she'd built so carefully around her emotions, in a rage of anger against the Fate that had snatched her lover from her.

Later, after the storm of weeping had passed, she found herself in a grove of ancient trees, several of which had fallen, ribbed and twisted, into swampy ground where they lay rotting. A skittering of little feet, several pairs of bright eyes and squiggles of black furry bodies chased each other around the trunks, pouring themselves in and out of its rotted holes – what were they – not squirrels, certainly. Anna laughed. They reminded her of Walt Disney films when cartoon creatures played around to make sad people happy again. There'd be bluebirds next. Through the archway of branches, she saw a single swan flying low over the Lake, black feet stretched out like water-skis, reaching for the surface. Sluicing heavily through the water, throwing up crystal spray, it sank to a more dignified posture, ruffling high white feathers into place like some duchess at a ball.

A trail of music wafted through the trees;

*'The silver swan who, living, hath no note,*
*When death approached unlock'd her silent throat.'*

Anna stood still, enthralled, as the great bird surged through a brush of fawn reeds like a galleon in full sail, one black eye gazing quizzically at her.

Feeling vaguely unnerved, she moved away, taking the shore path. You could walk right round the island in fifteen minutes, but she wasn't in a hurry. She trailed along, keeping thought at bay, breathing in dark aromas of decay from the boggy ground. Beyond the bristle of dead branches, over the smoothness of the Lake, mists seeped and swirled in slow motion so that there seemed to be no surrounding landscape, no context for the island, which floated alone, cocooned in soft grey cloud.

A cluster of scarlet toadstools spurted from the leaf-mould path. Anna stopped, shocked, for a moment seeing again the small red wound on Dave's temple that day in Paris, when she'd had to identify him in the morgue. Above her a rotting birch trunk split into a grin of frilled fungus. She quickened her pace. She didn't like this swampy place.

Would the bower still be there? With relief, she came upon the low stone wall encircling a knoll crowned with knotted bushes. Her feet remembered the secret path to its centre and she crept through, an arm over her face to fend off twigs. The smell, smokily pungent, whisked her back two months ago to the Loire, the formal gardens of a chateau – Chambord, Blois? The box hedges of the formal gardens there had smelled just like this. Two months.

It felt as though years had passed since she and Dave had taken the short holiday in August. The doctor had confirmed that her pregnancy was going well, and they had gone abroad to celebrate, for she had gone beyond the dangerous weeks. This time, unless Fate was once again to intervene, there would be a child. So many times their hopes had been dashed in the anguish of miscarriage. And now Dave himself was gone, victim of a terrorist's gun fired blindly in a Parisian street. She had been condemned to recover. For what? To live out her life without him?

A soft drizzle began to whisper through the tangle of branches. She could see the Lake through a gap in the trunks. A swag of heavier rain swept in on a shiver of wind, grizzling the surface, then a rush of droplets fell, blinding her briefly. Shaking the water out of her eyes, she saw the distant vapour resolve itself into the shape of the swan, breasting in to the little bay. It was keening a high fluting song. Then it wagged its head, ducking to dabble in the water for a crust someone had thrown.

A child stood on the shore, a little girl in fancy dress. She could have been four or five years old, and she was chattering to the swan in a high voice, in childish French. Her dark hair was caught into a rose-coloured satin snood, her long dress had high puffed shoulders, a tight waist and a little white ruff at the neck. She wore a black silk plaid fastened on the shoulder with a gold clasp. When the bread was finished, she turned, her long dark eyes staring directly at Anna. The intensity of her look seemed to say 'Come with me . . .' then she ran towards the sound of other children playing and laughing, the strumming of a guitar.

Something about the child's eyes, something she half-recognised, made Anna follow. Slithering a little on the steep path down the far side of the bower, she was amazed at the difference in this part of the island. The rain had stopped, and sunlight gilded low hazel bushes around an area of shorn grass. The path led her on to a knot-garden in which grew a tapestry of flowering herbs, each colour defined by neatly trimmed box hedges. Lavender, bay and rosemary spiced the air. Beyond, on a lawn, five little girls played under young apple-trees from which fruit hung in russset clusters. The tallest child was the one who had been feeding the swan.

A stately woman in dark Elizabethan costume called to her 'Marie', then bade each of the children in turn to hold hands around her. She strummed a lute while they began a

stately circular singing game, to the old madrigal Anna had
heard earlier. At the end, Marie sank down onto the ground,
enacting the part of the dying swan, as the others clapped
their hands.

A man strode across the lawn towards Anna, silhouetted
against the sun, a great scythe over his shoulder. Anna's heart
leapt. She started to run to him, knowing by his shape, the
square of his shoulders, the way he walked, that it was Dave.

But abruptly, he turned away, his face shrouded in the
cassock he wore. It was someone else, after all, a monk from
the Priory, a gardener sent out to cut the grass.
Disappointment rushed through her, unbearable in its
intensity.

'Brother McCurtain,' called the woman. 'Some hips and
haws, if you please, for the lasses to string.'

Mesmerised, Anna stood among the feathery branches of
a young cypress, incapable of rational thought, watching the
scene being played out. That this was some happening from
long ago she knew, yet did not question. She felt, in a way,
privileged to be there.

The monk returned to empty a spill of crimson berries
from the folds of his robe onto the ground beside the girls.
Sitting in a circle, they waited while the woman threaded
needles for each of them, then they began to string the fruits,
chattering as they worked. From the direction of the Priory
came a wail of chanting, lingering till it faded into the droning
of a late bee.

Mist swept across the garden again, blurring the
sunshine, dissolving all the people into grey shades as the rain
came on again. Feeling that she was an intruder, Anna
retreated towards the boxwood bower. But someone was
there already, half-visible. It was the child, Marie.

She stood staring out at Anna, long eyes grave in the pale
little face. A necklace of scarlet berries lay round her white
throat in a neat line above the ruff. Slowly she drew a hand
from behind her back. In it she held a white feather, and she

was clearly offering it to Anna.

Anna's eyes locked on the dreadful necklace, her mind frantically denying the horror of what it knew. A scream rising, she took the proffered feather. Then the gardener was there, dragging her through the bower, thrusting her out onto the muddy path beyond. A rushing wind spattered a drench of rain over her, and panic sent her running, pushing through undergrowth. Thorns tore at her clothes, branches grappled with her limbs – it was as if the island were trying to hold her there in the grip of its past.

Now she knew what her numbed mind had refused to acknowledge. That tainted child, Marie, was doomed to die, beheaded, on the scaffold. Some primeval instinct told Anna that if she didn't escape, the child within her would wither and die, cursed like the lives that had once been lived on this ancient island.

She fled round the shoreline, not stopping till she reached the custodian's hut. The Lake opened before her, half-hidden in coils of mist. Excalibur must have been reclaimed in such a place as this, she thought 'An arm clothed in white samite, mystic, wonderful.'

Behind her a dead leaf clattered down through the branches of the plane-tree. Remembering a childhood superstition, she moved to stand beneath the mossed and knotted boughs. To catch a falling leaf was to save a soul – and so brought good luck. The first one lay crumpled on the ground. Another fell, and she missed a further two. But the fifth she caught and held. Within her the babe fluttered, stirring for the first time. She had never felt such a marvellous sensation before.

From somewhere beyond the mist came the muffled stutter of the boat. In a few moments the hull materialised, its wake wobbling the dignified reflections of the Priory and its mournful cypresses as though they were insubstantial, transient as the mist.

The mirror-image of the swan sailed towards the jetty

through a diffusion of ripples, and for an instant its beady eye met hers. Then the great white bird took off, launching itself like some clumsy Concorde in a dazzle of spray. Anna marvelled at its strength – it needed every muscle to defy the pull of gravity, but nevertheless it soared into the air, to dispappear into the silver clouds.

'Used to be a pair,' said the boatman, holding out a hand to guide Anna on, and nodding in the direction of the vanished swan. 'I found the cob last winter. Shot. Poacher from the town after duck, likely. Swans have always belonged to Royalty, to the Queen. Folk say they mate for life. Oh, you've dropped your souvenirs.' He handed her the two long feathers. 'Pinions – wing-feathers. Without these the swan can't fly. After the moult it feels kind of low, but the feathers soon grow back in.'

The rag of brown land that was the island faded to fawn, then became one with the clouds as the boat slid across the Lake to where a bustle of wavelets slapped the mainland shore.